YELLOW TRAINS
TEN YEARS OF TESTING

YELLOW TRAINS
TEN YEARS OF TESTING

Andrew Royle

crecy.co.uk

In memory of Graeme Donald; a stalwart in the planning of these trains.

First published in 2019

© Andrew Royle 2019

A CIP record for this book is available from the British Library

Printed in Malta by Melita Press

ISBN 978 191080 9587

www.crecy.co.uk

Crécy Publishing Limited
1a Ringway Trading Estate, Shadowmoss Road,
Manchester M22 5LH
www.crecy.co.uk

Front cover: Views of the NMT between Swindon and Bristol (via Bath) proved difficult to obtain, as normally it would pass through after dark, even in high summer. However, in September 2014 a special series of runs were arranged with the hybrid set. 5 September 2014.

Back cover inset clockwise from top:
Heading a 1Z25 1436 Derby–Barrow Hill–Derby calibration run, 43013 sweeps through Duffield on a fine spring afternoon. 5 April 2006.

Underneath the NMT at Heaton to clean the cameras. 9 May 2011.

No. 37602 has reached Machen Quarry with RSC3. 18 August 2009.

Platform 6 at Liverpool's Lime Street station finds 43014 enjoying the sunshine before returning to Crewe. 8 April 2009.

Back cover main: No. 73138 (with 73107 at rear) pauses with a rake of coaches that includes TRC at Kilburn High Road working 1Q76, the 2143 Selhurst–Selhurst, via Watford Junction. 12 February 2011.

Contents

At the south end of Crewe station, we have two trains working back to Derby: NMT has just arrived from Carlisle, while 97301 is leaving with a returning shakedown run of the Electrification Monitoring Vehicle 977983 (EMV). 4 May 2011.

Introduction

At the turn of the millennium, I was working in Nottingham as a computer programmer on the railway seat reservation system. Having failed to find a way into British Rail employment from school in the mid-1980s, I'd trained as a programmer with the MoD and after some years working in other transport sectors, finally managed to get into the post-privatisation railway on the strength of that experience. In January 2000, people talked about re-evaluating their lives and careers and, somewhat unintentionally, I was about to do just that. I'd had enough of spending most of my working life sitting in an office in front of a screen; I'd look outside on sunny days and wonder whether there was a better working life to be had, while I was still young enough to enjoy it. No doubt many others have wondered just the same! One morning before leaving for work, I resolved to call a halt to the misery of knowing things weren't going to change anytime soon.

This book is mainly a summary of the work I went on to do as an on-train technician (OTT) for Network Rail between 2002 and 2012. Although my account is written in the past tense, much of the work of the infrastructure monitoring fleet at the time of writing is similar, though for how much longer that will be the case remains to be seen, such is technological progress. I took my camera with me wherever I went and (work and safety permitting), I recorded views of the trains, the equipment and the people involved in running a vital part of network operations. Whilst the majority of the photos were taken during the period in question, I've allowed myself the liberty of including a few others from after that time when I was a fleet engineer. I have also tried to put together a selection that concentrates on depot or station locations, rather than the usual lineside views.

I would like to thank Arthur Richards in particular for his assistance in the production of this book – he was a leading light in the development of track recording systems in the 1970s. Apologies to the many drivers, technicians, engineers and support staff who I worked with that have escaped a mention, I trust you will enjoy reading this anyway!

The conference room in 975814, NMT.

Preparing for the Role

I think it was in *Railnews* that I spotted the advert from Omnicom Engineering in York looking for technicians to help with the contract they'd won from Railtrack to carry out a video survey of the entire network. There was nothing too specific about experience but, as luck would have it, the man interviewing me had worked for BR Business Systems (as I recently had) and he seemed keen enough to take me on. A group of us gathered in a small upstairs office in Micklegate to hear what we'd be doing and I knew then that I'd hit on something good, even if the money was nothing to write home about – who cared? For the next two years, I acted as a technician onboard the single unit DMU number 960011 (a.k.a. *Pandora*) that Balfour Beatty had fitted out, in collaboration with Omnicom.

Pandora waits at Nairn during one of its grand tours of Scotland; the two signal boxes at either end of the platform here had only recently ceased operation and were both boarded up. Unit number 960011 also carried the stock number 977859 and in BR days was W55025. Stuart Smith, the Balfour Beatty train planner who drew up the train's surveying schedule, recalled going to Bridport on it in the 1960s. Little did I know then that I would be back here seven years later on board the TRU. 14 October 2001.

On 18 April 2007, Track Inspection Coach DB999508 (better known as TIC) sits in the RTC yard at Derby. Originally an area manager's inspection saloon on the Western Region (pictures exist of it working a final train to Ilfracombe in 1975), it was taken into the test train fleet and modified with the indented side window arrangement. With the two spot lamps mounted underneath, this created a lookout position for the track recorder who needed to see where the mileposts were and also which track his train was taking in good time. The far end saloon was used for storage.

This job served as an introduction to life at the sharp end of the railway. Not only did I experience how train planning for out-of-the-ordinary working took place but I saw first-hand how a train was managed and driven on the network, all useful knowledge for what was to come. One of the Omnicom technician's roles was to sit in the front seat of the DMU to provide a running commentary on the infrastructure being videoed and to help ensure it stayed on the correct route. From this viewpoint, the thing that struck me was how there were always so many parties involved; so many elements to get right and numerous items of equipment to function correctly on the day, not to mention the part that the weather would often play. We relied on conductors practically everywhere we went and one 'no show' could lead to cancellation of a whole day's work – work that sometimes wasn't easily replanned.

We witnessed all manner of unusual things from the train during that project. Entering the Kyle of Lochalsh station area, our conductor detrained to rescue a young Japanese tourist who had wandered past us, apparently looking for the way out from the station. Still in Scotland, another conductor's wife and daughter came out to meet us at Keith station with milk when we'd mentioned to him that we were running low; somehow I couldn't

imagine that happening in many other parts of the country. And one thing I certainly couldn't imagine happening anywhere was the time that a signaller stepped out from his box and dropped his trousers in full view of the train's cameras. That didn't occur on my shift, I'm somewhat relieved to report. Then a driver who we used temporarily in the London area decided to stop *Pandora* on the Hornsey Flyover mid-recording to lean out and pick cherries from a tree that was overhanging the line there. He said he'd had his eye on them for ages! One of the funniest sights I can remember, although off the railway, was the sequence of three shop fronts close to Three Bridges station in Crawley: A Chinese takeaway, a chemist and a funeral directors.

I also got to hear the stories that were shared between the drivers and conductors, often concerning the frustrations they'd experienced with unsympathetic management or an ignorant public. Driver Bob Cox (who we referred to as 'Biggles', as he also had a pilot's licence) once drove for Connex and recounted the occasion when he'd received permission to pass a signal at danger at a time when SPADs had been in the news. This had clearly been observed by a lady passenger, leaning out of the window of the EMU he'd been driving, because she got off at the next

The NMT's power cars were ready some months before the rest of the train and 43013/62 came down to the RTC from Neville Hill for initial assessment by the technical staff there. At this stage, they carried a slightly different set of markings, to what they were to carry, once in normal service. On Saturday, 15 February 2003, the two work as 0Z16 Etches Park–Doncaster past Spondon on their way to join the stock at Wabtec's facility. The juxtaposition with the yellow plant nearby wasn't planned!

station and banged on his droplight window to say she was going to report him for it. When he told her he'd been given permission by the signalman, she said she'd report the signalman as well. 'Yes, madam, you do that!' was Bob's reply and up went the droplight. I was told that he had previously flown Boeing 737s in the U.S. – quite a difference to a Class 121 DMU!

In the end, we didn't quite manage to capture video footage of every running line. One or two branch lines proved a little too elusive, what with the worsening problem of a lack of daytime train paths on certain single lines, coupled with the need to arrange for a conductor to be present on the pre-arranged day; so many things needed to come together for a successful 'hit' and the requirement for quality video footage of the most important routes seemed to take priority over closing out every last mile on the railway map. The combination of the video recordings, the positional GPS data that was gathered and the Omnicom software went to produce a safer desktop method of planning that reduced the need for people to go out on the track. In 2018, I heard that some of that information we'd produced more than fifteen years earlier was still being used!

So my two years with Omnicom was time well spent. Then, another advert in *Railnews* from Serco Railtest Ltd

caught my eye, this time looking for rail-experienced staff to boost their team of on-train technicians. It was only after I'd applied that I discovered they particularly wanted people to work on the New Measurement Train (NMT), Network Rail's solution to a need for stepping up the level of track monitoring on principal routes in the aftermath of the Hatfield accident.

One former colleague of mine from Omnicom, Andy Morris, had already joined ahead of me and the good news I received from him was that the pay was rather better. Having successfully interviewed at the Railway Technical Centre in Derby, I just needed to take an aptitude test. This was the one that they used for drivers: testing your eyesight, spatial awareness, recognition of fault patterns, etc. I passed it easily. We then underwent full training as train guards, undertaking classroom sessions at the old LMS training school along London Road on railway operations, signalling, shunting, first aid/ firefighting and how to act if first on the scene of an accident. I found the toughest part was proving I could lift the heavy buckeye coupler on a coach from the stowed to the service position unassisted. This was one of those activities that, if you didn't master the right technique, meant you wasted most of your energy if you couldn't insert the pin on the first or second time of asking! I found that the trick was to swing the coupler up on to your hip (ouch!) with your stronger arm and reach for the pin on the end of its chain with the other. Then it was one last heave to get the coupler horizontal before quickly slipping the pin into the hole to lock it in place. Luckily for me, we had a very patient instructor.

Learning our 'rules and regs' took some time too … unless your name was Kevin Smith and you had a photographic memory for the detail. Time was spent sitting in the control office and in the planning department as well, so that we gained a proper appreciation of how it all came together on the day. Knowing who you were speaking to on the phone might not seem such an issue but it was that attention to detail in the training that, looking back, helped to make all the difference, especially once you were out on your own.

It became apparent that the NMT wouldn't be ready for service as early as had been hoped, so come October 2002 the trainee OTTs began to be sent out on the existing monitoring fleet to gain some useful experience. I went out on the Structure Gauging Train (SGT) first with Rob Clamp and Graham Wildgoose, followed by a couple of days on the Track Recording Coach (TRC) with John Braiden and Naz Jacob. Following a health and safety

review, sleeping onboard the trains was just coming to an end, though not before I had spent my first night on TRC trying to get some sleep whilst stabled in front of Carlisle signal box. There, of course, freight trains kept running by all night and the Class 92s that passed felt like they were going to join me in my compartment!

Having learned about the track recording process itself in Trent House, I was sent out on the Track Inspection Coach (TIC) to learn my trade properly with Stuart Bradshaw and Phil McDermott. Thankfully they were perfectly happy to pass on their knowledge in a constructive and helpful manner (not always the case in the railway industry), even though they knew I would be working exclusively on the NMT and unlikely to be returning the favour, seeing as everyone was allocated to only one train at that time. I'd heard that one or two others hadn't had the best of experiences on another train. Whilst TRC and the Track Recording Unit (TRU) had been built specifically with track recording in mind, TIC was something of a cobbled together affair inasmuch as whilst the modifications made to it were obvious, it still exhibited many features left over from its previous roles as an inspection saloon and also a video survey vehicle. None of it was ergonomically planned or indeed particularly safe – lots of sharp edges for one thing and the inset

The higher of the red notices reads 'Crew Asleep, Contact 01332 262338'. The idea was that, should the train need to be moved (by that class 08, for example!), then a phone call to Control in Derby ought to be made before banging on the window of Radio Survey DMU *Iris II*. Being awake before my colleagues in the dormitory at the far end (in RDB977693), I've crept out to take a few photos at Old Oak Common depot. RDB977694 is at this end – the 'RDB' was dropped on repainting into NR yellow livery. 13 March 2003.

The New Measurement Train is seen at 'Four Shed', Derby Etches Park shortly before leaving for Darlington on its first full test run as 1Z82 0900 to Darlington. Several things are noted here: a difference in shade of yellow paint can be detected between the side of the train and its front warning panel area. There is a beading (wooden, I think) running around the side of the nose of 43062 below the headlight boxes; I never found out what this was for or whether other power cars ever had it. The wipers have yet to be fitted to the camera box. In the right background can be seen ex-Southern Region de-icing coach 975600 (from set 930010) that was in use as a site office and store. These sidings were later redeveloped into a covered maintenance facility for Meridian DMUs. 9 May 2003.

observation windows where the track recording technician sat was regarded by some as a likely crumple zone in the event of a serious accident, the unfortunate technician becoming the meat in the sandwich! If it was fine with a crew of just two, it was perhaps a bit of a crowd in there with three. I didn't know it then but I would come to spend quite a bit of time on TIC in the ensuing years.

Come March 2003, the NMT's power cars had appeared in Derby for initial assessment. However, the finished product was still some months away so my next entertainment was a few trips on *Iris II*, the two-car DMU used for radio survey work. Successor to the original Derby Lightweight single unit *Iris*, this was a self-contained working entity in a similar vein to the TRU; a considerably older and less comfortable one, though … One car was the

working area while the other was a dormitory with beds separated by curtains. Too bad if anyone was a loud snorer!

I could see that the novelty of sleeping on board a train between shifts would wear thin with me. Alright, you didn't need to worry about getting to work of a morning but you could never escape from it properly at the end of a long day either. And if you didn't really enjoy the company of any colleague, that might also be an issue. I had been quite pleased to hear that on the NMT we would always be using hotels when staying away from home. The unknown quantity would be the times and duration of the shifts we'd be given on what was becoming an increasingly congested network.

Before relating any further experiences, I shall outline the work itself in a little more detail.

While undergoing a general induction into the role of an OTT, I was sent out with Graham Wildgoose and Rob Clamp on the Structure Gauging Train (when it ran as a train in its own right). Four-wheel wagon No. DC460000 (constructed in 1982) was the heart of the train, seen here at Didcot on 17 October 2002. An array of white lights in the central slot shone outwards onto the surrounding infrastructure, to then be videoed by the cameras mounted at the ends of the indented section (the port holes were used as a means of checking the light array during running).

Nicknamed 'The Rocket' (I can't recall why), DB975081 was the DVT for the SGT (37710 provided the power on this trip). Previously Lab 17 *Hermes*, this was actually never an SR EMU driving vehicle (despite appearances!) but a modified Mark 1 BSK. 17 October 2002.

The Track Recording Process

Monitoring of track alignment is principally for safety reasons, namely the prevention of track faults developing to the extent that they might cause a derailment. However it is also to enhance passenger comfort and to reduce wear and tear on rolling stock. Without going into lengthy detail, the greater your investment in track maintenance and monitoring effort, in theory the higher your standard of track should be. The most important geometry features that can lead to derailment are wide gauge (distance between rails greater than the standard 1435mm), track twist (where one rail dips relative to the other, leading to the risk of a wheel flange climbing over the top of the rail) and cyclic top (a 'roller coaster' effect in the longitudinal profile of the track that can lead to a build-up of vertical energy in the suspension of vehicles until they bounce off it). Other features such as poor alignment (snaking track) and dipped joints (at rail joints or welds) were also assessed. The actual causes of such faults ranged from failing track components (damaged sleepers, dislodged track clips or worn rail pads) to insufficient or contaminated ballast and subsidence of the formation.

While waiting to proceed back to Inverness from Georgemas Jn, on this occasion there was ample time for the TRU crew to stretch their legs; a peaceful location and not a passenger in sight. 8 July 2008.

The view from TIC 999508 when working between 31602 (pictured) and 31459 in South Yorkshire. By this time, only two printers were in use: the action printer on the left, reporting on track faults, and the trace printer on the right, which printed track alignment traces for every mile recorded. Other items on view are Quail maps, a roll of heavy tissue paper (always useful), stapler, track manual and clipboard with train timing sheets. What the extension lead was for, I don't recall but we were all issued with one of those classic Nokia mobile phones. The cameras were left over from a video survey project some years previously and not functioning, just like the windscreen wipers! 2 March 2010.

I would say that checking track alignment (or geometry) is at the heart of what the test train fleet is used for. It has the longest history, as track recording cars have been in use since at least the early days of British Rail, when poor alignment was marked by dropping doses of paint into the four foot for the benefit of the track gangs. Much of what follows may still apply but when I joined Serco, the track recording vehicles TRC and TRU had pressurised equipment linked to the Track Geometry Computer (TGC) that automatically fired a shot of red dye mixture vertically downwards whenever a severe fault was detected. Rather temperamental in operation (the nozzle often got blocked), its use was phased out when more accurate GPS-based reporting of fault locations was established. I was tasked with drawing up a procedure for its operation and routine maintenance not long before the decision to stop using it was made. Oh well … at least nobody needed to manhandle those drums of dye around anymore, often spilling it everywhere!

A sliding scale of fault reporting was used: most events could safely be written to file and reported to the track maintaining group at the end of the recording shift, while more serious ones were either deemed as 'thirty-six-hour' faults (which needed calling in straightaway) or 'close the line'. The latter required the onboard team to make a

sharp assessment of the track geometry traces on the computer printout as to whether the fault reading was genuine and then get the driver to stop the train immediately so that the signaller could be contacted to block all traffic over the affected section. An inspection or repair by the track maintainers would be needed before traffic could be allowed to run again. I personally only had to close the line once in ten years whilst working the NMT (track twist on a heavily used section of pointwork at Sheffield station) but on TRU, which was tasked with checking minor routes and freight-only lines on a less frequent basis, this was quite a regular occurrence.

So how were the track faults detected? The Serco-Lewis Digital Track Geometry System (DTGS) was in operation on TRC, TRU and TIC when I joined; a combination of the onboard TGC being fed measurements from a low-power laser measuring system and an inertial measuring unit of accelerometers and gyroscopes, linked to an arrangement of body and bogie-mounted transducers that showed how the vehicle pitched, swayed and rolled over the track. The less they moved, the better the condition of the track! A further feed of data was the set of 'RSTs', Route Setting Tapes that were compiled for every route. Stored originally on physical reel-to-reel computer tapes, these were now

Close-up of a transducer on one of the NMT Mark 3's bogies. Otherwise known as an LVDT (Linear Variable Differential Transformer), this fed information about the vertical movement of the coach into the onboard computers.

The ImageMap track traces as the NMT approaches Stafford South Junction on the down main. While the traces appear erratic, they aren't a literal interpretation of the track but actually represent quite a sensitive measurement of its geometry. The list of individual traces is shown on the right: The ninth and tenth (cross level and curvature) show that the train is coming off the Queensville Curve and on to the straighter track at the junction. Where these two traces slope, the track is in transition from the curve to the straight and the designed increased track twist around mileage 133/1 (which is intended) can be seen on the first trace.

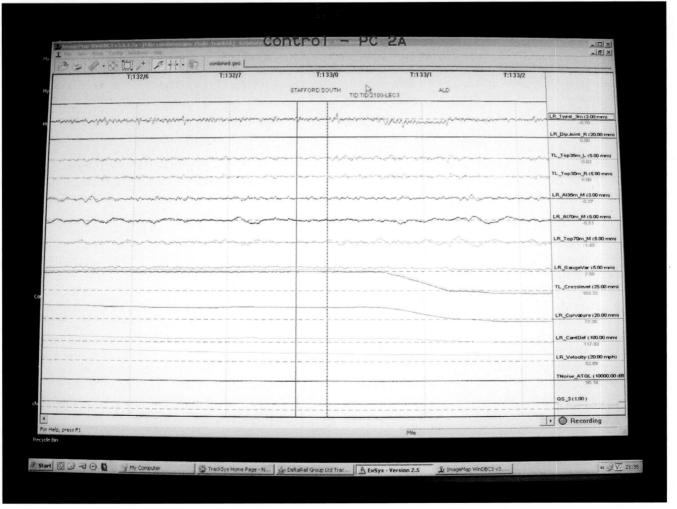

No. 31233 has just tailed the TRC set into platform 19 at Waterloo, headed by 73107 (then named *Spitfire*). I suspect that 73138 was the usual partner loco but had to be replaced by the 31 for some reason. I was down in London ready to work the NMT to Plymouth the following day (Friday) and had gone here just to take a photo. Having walked back to the other end to say hello to the crew though, I found myself agreeing to man the train to Selhurst Depot while they hot-footed it down to the tube to get an earlier service train home; their working week was done! 22 April 2010.

data files that held information about the specific track being monitored. The TGC needed to assess the track differently according to the ruling line speed. For example, there needed to be a more stringent assessment of a 125mph main line than that for a 20mph freight-only branch. RSTs could cover recording runs of just a half mile curve or a 100+ mile journey along one of the main lines. They tended to be written to suit the schedules obtained at the planning stage with the aim of having a string of line information that could most easily be applied to a recording train's journey, without having to stop it at an operationally inconvenient location prior to any run. There might be overlapping RSTs on some routes. For example, there might be one from Stratford-upon-Avon to Hatton Station but also one to use for Stratford to Hatton North Junction, depending on what timings had been obtained.

It also had to be borne in mind that full dynamic geometry data could only be recorded above a minimum of about 15mph. For example, cyclic top could only be assessed with the train's transducers undergoing some degree of vertical motion. And the dynamic aspect of the operation was important because you were carrying out

measurements of the track with the weight of a train on it, thus giving more realistic data.

At the beginning of every monitoring shift, the Optel laser system needed warming up and benchmarking on a reasonably straight piece of track to (hopefully) find the correct measuring points on the inside of the crown of each rail. If the train had been stabled on a time-served and uneven old siding then the process could be tricky. 'CAUTION, LASER ACTIVATED' was the sound of the muffled recording broadcast repeatedly outside the coach whilst doing this, the idea being to deter anyone coming too close and potentially be affected by the laser, which would normally only work whilst the train was in motion. The area underneath the bogie where the lasers were mounted was shrouded by heavy rubber guards intended to stop extraneous light entering the measuring area and interfering with the measurement. At times the only way to persuade the lasers to find the correct measure points was for someone to stand outside the train, hold their foot against the rubber guard and wait for the thumbs-up from inside. I recall doing this in a platform at Kings Cross once with dozens of commuters walking past and clearly

Platform 6 at Liverpool's Lime Street station finds 43014 enjoying the sunshine before returning to Crewe. At this time, the NMT would make two return trips between Crewe and Liverpool in order to record the fast lines and the slows between Ditton Junction and Wavertree. 8 April 2009.

wondering what was going on! The rubber guards weren't 100 per cent effective: in winter when the sun was low in the sky, sunlight would sometimes manage to shine through the small gap between guard and rail. One such occasion was near Ivybridge (on a curved section of the Devon main line) when the computer suddenly produced a series of warnings that said we should close the line because of wide gauge. Inspection of the track geometry traces on the printout showed these were false. The experience of the technicians came into play here but if there was a 'cliff face' or spike in the trace then that was usually the giveaway. It was nigh on impossible for track gauge to change instantly by 30–40mm; our train would already be derailed if it had. Gauge spikes were common when the train passed over pointwork and the laser detected the gap in the rails.

OK, so let's say our equipment has measured correctly and declared it has found a 'thirty-six-hour' fault, that being the length of time within which the fault has to be corrected. Fine, but obviously we need to be able to tell the maintainers exactly where that fault is – they don't want to be wandering up and down near such-and-such a station or whatever level crossing looking for it, we have to tell them to the nearest chain where it is. Before pinpoint accurate GPS became available, the technicians had to keep the computer 'in sync' with the train's position on the

network and that meant with the lineside mileposts at every quarter of a mile. Any track recording run would be started by a hand-held push button, which set the TGC running at a pre-determined milepost in accordance with the appropriate RST that had been loaded into the program. The exact circumference of the wheels on the measuring bogie would also be loaded (the tachometer count figure) so that the computer would report all data in the correct position, using the rotations of the wheel. A loud beep would sound every eighth of a mile covered and therefore each time a milepost was passed. That sounds simple enough but the crew needed to keep an eye on the synchronisation continually. Some mileposts aren't placed where they ought to be and, whilst those inaccuracies should have been incorporated into the RST, there would always be the odd one or two that hadn't. Furthermore, if the wheels of the train were wearing down, or if they'd been turned on a wheel lathe recently, then the tachometer figure might no longer be accurate, leading to a drift in the synchronisation. The technician working the computer would have to occasionally resync the computer using the push-button at a reliable milepost, not easy at speed or in the dark, or both. Oh yes, and mileposts aren't always there at all (some proving too attractive to collectors, perhaps?) and they don't all look the same. Further, axle counter 'mushrooms' look very similar to mileposts when you pass them at speed or in the dark … or both! Some are down in the cess, others halfway up the side of a cutting or fixed to a retaining wall. Certain Scottish ones reminded me of 'clubs' in a pack of cards. Most OTTs had their own horror stories of trying to get a sync done when the odds were against them. But if the tachometer count was accurate then you could expect to travel upwards of 40 miles before needing to consider a resync. The TIC had well-placed external lights to help see mileposts at night, whereas TRC's were poor and always seemed to get dirty or damaged too easily. In the early days of running TRC in the NMT formation, we took to using a powerful torch out of a droplight window, one

technician having to shout 'NOW!' to the other at the computer, telling him when to press the resync button.

Each track recording vehicle would consume huge quantities of multi-part and A4 paper as the track maintainers always wanted printouts of the track traces and reportable faults for their area. There were normally three printers: An action printer listing all the actionable faults (from those that needed attention within ten days to those that required closing of the line – see figure A), a Standard Deviation printer (which printed out SD values for every eighth of a mile, giving an idea of overall track quality) plus an A4 printer showing the 'wigglies' – track traces

```
TRACK RECORDING for NetworkRail by SERCO RAILTEST
TRACK RECORDING VEHICLE [NMT] [SL_DTGS V5.04]               AREA [ WCML - 21A          ]
ACTION REPORT          Page 004 Date 1- 3-2005             ZONE [ LONDON NORTH WEST     ]
JOURNEY: EUSTON TO LIVERPOOL LIME ST VIA DOWN SLOW - LINE <C>  0016/1   PWME [ PWME SOUTH          ]
PWSS: PWSM BLETCHLEY          ELRX: LEC1 2200              FILE [ NMTTU0501030521A     ]
_____

Location        Level  Dist   Channel   Peak    Line      Action          Sign-off
Miles yds ch            AWSm            Value   Speed


CHEDDINGTON STATION
  37m 871y(39)    ( 30)  947    GAUGE    33.2mm [ 90]  Inspect within 36hours > :_____:___/___/___

Manual resync(R) to 40/0 (27y)
LEIGHTON BUZZARD STATION
START OF LINSLADE CENTRE BORE <UP FAST/D
END OF LINSLADE CENTRE BORE <UP FAST/D
  46/4 - 46/5 SD1(3.1)      ALIG35    3.7mm [ 75]                  > :_____:___/___/___

BLETCHLEY STATION
  46/5 - 46/6 SD1(5.7)      AL70      5.9mm [ 75]                  > :_____:___/___/___

  46/7 - 47/0 SD1(4.0)      LTOP      4.5mm [ 90]                  > :_____:___/___/___

  46/7 - 47/0 SD1(4.0)      RTOP      4.9mm [ 90]                  > :_____:___/___/___

  46/7 - 47/0 SD1(5.6)      MT70      6.6mm [ 90]                  > :_____:___/___/___

    47m 669y(30)  C      307  CYC9_LT = 18.1mm [ 90]  D (Correct  :120days) > :_____:___/___/___
           to  47m 720y(33): 3 cycles
  47/3 - 47/4 SD1(2.7)      ALIG35    3.1mm [ 90]                  > :_____:___/___/___

  47/3 - 47/4 SD1(5.6)      MT70      5.9mm [ 90]                  > :_____:___/___/___

  47/3 - 47/4 SD1(5.0)      AL70      5.9mm [ 90]                  > :_____:___/___/___

  47/5 - 47/6 SD1(5.6)      MT70      6.9mm [ 90]                  > :_____:___/___/___

MILTON KEYNES CENTRAL STATION
WOLVERTON STATION
HANSLOPE JN <SLOW LINE - N'TH'TON
ELRX: HNR  2100
  56m 915y(41)    ( 15)  772    ALIG35   19.3mm [ 75]        10 Days > :_____:___/___/___

  56m 915y(41)    ( 30)  772    GAUGE    40.9mm [ 75]  Inspect within 36hours > :_____:___/___/___

  56m1146y(52)    (-15)  983    ALIG35  -16.0mm [ 75]        10 Days > :_____:___/___/___



    Signature PWSM _____   Date returned to PWME _____/_____/_____
```

Figure A

for gauge, cant, alignment, etc. The multi-part printers were prone to jamming whenever the perforated paper margin holes slipped on the printer sprockets; you had to be quick to spot this happening or you might end up with a chewed bit of rubbish with a thick black line of unreadable information across it.

At the end of the shift, all the paper had to be processed into neat bundles for each of the track maintainers who had an interest in that shift's recording. If you'd been doing the Far North line from Inverness, for example, then only one group might be involved, so sorting was easy. If the train had started in South Wales and taken a circuitous route back to Derby through the Midlands, several piles needed creating. Some technicians preferred to lay it all out on the floor of the coach in an effort to get this right – not so easy in the cramped confines of TIC! With a weighing scale and a large stock of stamps kept onboard, the usual procedure was to pack it all up into large envelopes and look to find a pillar box to post the printouts after the shift. However, some track engineers liked to ride the train through their patch and asked to take theirs away with them. Others would phone the train and ask us to drop the paperwork off to someone waiting at a station; shades of the old postal mail drops whenever we didn't actually need to stop to make the handover!

You could expect to be busier on the TRU, bearing in mind the nature of the routes that it covered and the fact that they generally weren't monitored as frequently as the main lines were covered by the NMT. It wasn't unusual for an NMT shift to pass without having to call in any reportable faults. I recall being on and off the phone for almost an entire TRU shift in the South Yorkshire area once: By the time I'd noted the details of a fault in the log and called it in, the train had moved on and detected another two or three. It was helpful to have someone in fault control who was used to the routine, of course – one poor chap in an area fault control office, clearly unused to this, got so uptight from the quantity of faults we were having to call in that he told us to stop ringing him! That wasn't an option, of course, so the faults were passed to the national control office for processing. When NMT took over recording of the Settle and Carlisle line from TRU, it was at a time when coal traffic was starting to boom on the route and the older stretches of jointed track

This view shows the Laserail camera assembly on one side of the Production Vehicle 977994. The laser shines on to the rail from the circular enclosure at the top (with two compressed air pipes, to help reduce dirt ingress) while the four cameras in the other enclosure (angled, with four air pipes) inspect its reflection on the rail. Together with the image feed from the other side, this provided data to assess track geometry. A black rubber shroud (to prevent interference from incidental light) is visible at bottom left. One of the OTT's jobs at the start of the day was to get underneath the vehicle to clean the laser and camera enclosures.

still remaining were suffering. A number of faults were picked up but coming south over Ais Gill you couldn't get a mobile phone signal until you reached Settle Junction, so it got a little uncomfortable having to wait to phone them in; any delay was to be avoided as it reduced the time window for fixing any faults.

Single-track branch lines were almost always recorded on the outward run (that was how the RST was usually compiled), picking up any passing loops on the return. The only problem with that approach was the danger of finding a 'close the line' fault on the way out and then be stuck the wrong side of it whilst the maintainers checked or corrected it.

During 2005, a new track recording system was introduced on to NMT by the substitution of TRC with PV (Production Vehicle). The new system was known as Tracksys and was designed to be guided by RTPS (Real Time Positioning System), a kind of satnav that always knew which track the train was running on. That would make everyone's life a lot easier – sounds great, doesn't it? Unfortunately the new system took a very long time to become reliable and the technicians were kept busy overriding it. Most frustrating of all was that it was more inaccurate in the places where you needed it most, such as complex junctions and approaches to large stations. You would often find a number of small alignment faults here and they all needed calling in, so the skill and judgment of the technician was as important as ever. Tracksys had a screen front end that would often freeze mid-run. The loud beep of Serco-Lewis that sounded every eighth of a mile had

Above: Nos 67006 and 67016 power an audit run of TIC (rear coach) from the RTC to Barrow Hill. EWS drivers who didn't regularly drive test trains could make life interesting for us at times, especially those who just got in the cab and set off when they were ready. At the start of a shift, one colleague once left the recording coach at a siding to give the necessary handheld radio to the driver for communication, only to see the train accelerate away without him. All sorts of liveries are evident in this photo. Note also the semi-derelict shed in the top left of shot, which housed a withdrawn (and equally derelict) 08536 for several years before it was demolished. 17 March 2004.

Overleaf: Derby station sees a visit from the UFM160 track recording unit, probably to carry out the same calibration tests that the rest of the NR track recording vehicles had to perform periodically. Plasser & Theurer built this DMU and (in conjunction with Eurailscout and Carillion) had a contract to carry out track monitoring on the Southern zone for a time. This was entirely separate to the Serco operation that I was involved in, by this time taken in house by Network Rail. Numbered 999700/1, it eventually returned to the Continent, as NR decided to use TRC in its place. 22 March 2006.

been replaced by an electronic 'bong' and if that suddenly stopped you knew Tracksys was in trouble. At first, we tended to panic and restart the whole recording process, something that took several minutes to do, during which time all recording data was lost. But after a while it was realised that this wasn't necessary; the problem was just with the front end and recording was still taking place in the background. Whilst taking a few minutes to achieve, restarting the front end was comical though as the system would then catch up on all the 'bongs' required for the distance covered in the interim. It would go crazy:

B-b-b-b-b-bo-b-bo-bo-bo-bo-bo-bong. B-b-bong.
Bo-bo-bo-bong-bong. Bo-bo-bong.

Bong

Bong

Bong

Ah, there we go. Back to normal now and no recording lost. Put the kettle on, somebody! We need a coffee to celebrate.

Audit runs (or 'cal' runs) were conducted annually, over a period of about a fortnight or so, each spring. Whenever a track recording vehicle was off the network for heavy maintenance, the measuring equipment on each train was calibrated 'on the bench' by the technical support team. But the 'cal' runs were done as a comparison among whichever vehicles were in the fleet at the time, namely TRC, NMT, TIC, TRU and SMT (the Southern Measurement Train or UFM160). The latter was a Plasser-built two-car DMU operated by one of the infrastructure maintenance companies on a trial basis, mostly on third-rail territory. NR-employed staff never got to work on it and we tended not to have much to do with those who did, only encountering them in the RTC canteen occasionally. How successful its recording methodology turned out none of us discovered but when the trial came to an end, the unit returned to the Continent and its duties passed back to TRC once again, now that the latter had been released from use as part of the NMT formation.

Anyway, each recording vehicle (in its usual operating formation) would be taken up to Barrow Hill sidings and then run over a 5-mile section of the up main from the south end of Clay Cross Tunnel, the general idea being that if similar results were obtained across the fleet then all was well! Not the most scientific method of doing it, it seemed to me, but my job wasn't really to question the approach. Recording had to be done in both forward and reverse at differing speeds, so 'cal' runs were typically done as follows: 7 runs at 20, 30, 45, 60, 70, 80 and 90 on one day; then the same again the next day though with an earlier start time from Derby to include a run out via Spondon, Trent Junction and the Erewash Valley line in order to turn the train beforehand.

Now that seems fine on paper but it has to be borne in mind that Clay Cross Junction to Derby isn't exactly the quietest part of the network, so we had to mix it with all the regular freight and passenger services. Whilst we had special timings to take into account the varying speeds, things just never seemed to go to plan. Running at 20mph over 5 miles, for instance, practically amounts to taking a short possession of the route and the driver had to clear this first with Sheffield power box if he didn't want to incur their wrath when a late-running Virgin Voyager found itself behind us. Similarly, there were times when we set out to do the 90mph run only to sight yellow signals approaching the junction because matey had decided to put a freight across in front of us! One year there was even a TSR in place at the north end of the tunnel so, with something of a climb up to the tunnel mouth to boot, even a 2+5 HST set could not achieve the full 90 by the start of the test site. The instruction to the driver in that case was to hold whatever speed that could be attained as constant speed was the crucial thing here. Some drivers were better than others at achieving this …

On one occasion, there was consternation in the office at how the data from one vehicle seemed to differ markedly from all the others. Further enquiries, however, revealed that this last set of tests had taken place after a weekend and, sure enough, it transpired that the local maintainers had been busy with their tamper on the Sunday!

I was told that in past years the test track at Old Dalby had been used for the 'cal' runs but, with that now in somebody else's hands and not inconsiderable sums required for its use, Railtrack in their wisdom had decided to use the national network for the job. This struck me as an unwelcome extra burden for the already busy Derby and Sheffield signal box staff, as well as a waste of fuel involved in the unproductive shuttling back and forth between Derby and Chesterfield. A return to Old Dalby was made some years later!

A day's 'cal' runs was normally covered by two shifts: The first taking it off the RTC or Etches Park around 0700–0730 with the second shift joining them at around 1300 for the fourth run of the day. This allowed for a healthy exchange of views on how things were going and a leisurely handover of the baton, as it were. The favourite place (for the signaller) to stick the train during layovers was the carriage siding alongside platform 6 at Derby but if we were lucky we might get a platform proper, which permitted a quick dash to the station buffet for sandwiches. These trips were also a chance for office-based staff to come aboard and appreciate what sort of problems could arise on the train. It was just a pity that certain decision-makers in the organisation rarely seemed to take advantage of this.

Short-notice 'cal' runs could also get arranged to prove the working of an item of equipment and on one occasion I was asked to take out the TIC alone on a Friday evening to do a run at 90mph and another at 20mph. I recall indicating to one of the technical support staff (Rob Smith) that I wasn't feeling very confident about it, so he kindly offered to accompany me on the first run. Although he wasn't a trained OTT, he was familiar with the equipment so that gave me a bit of a confidence boost. That was actually the

Nos 73141 *Charlotte* and 73212, seen with TRC during a lunch break at Ascot. At this stage, TRC had recently reassumed responsibility for track recording on ex-Southern third rail territory. The very clean ex-Royal Train escort coach 977969 is behind 73141; there were still some police transfers to be seen on one of the internal compartment windows. 26 May 2010.

kind of thing that I look back on with great pride; the fact that teams worked together and supported each other. They didn't feel the need to point the finger or rush to judgement on others in order to make themselves feel superior (as I later found to be the case in other parts of the business, sadly). Being somewhat out of practice at the time, both at doing a 'cal' run and operating this aged vehicle, I didn't quite complete the high-speed run correctly. Not that it mattered so much – one of the top-and-tail Class 37 locos wasn't producing power when required and the signaller joined in the fun by giving us yellows so we only managed 60mph on exit from the tunnel! The slow-speed run was better (completely on my own this time) and sufficient to prove the equipment was working as it should.

OTTs tended to only work one type of train initially – it was just the NMT for me at first – so they became accustomed to the routine of things and they knew where the awkward mileposts were or where poor-quality track was likely to be. One location at the south end of Preston station always seemed to produce the same thirty-six-hour reportable fault. Then there was a move to spread the knowledge around a bit more, so for a time everyone could be expected to work across the whole fleet of trains, whilst keeping one as their core working platform. That was fine in principle but it led to a deterioration in the quality of the data produced at times, as people found themselves on routes with which they weren't familiar; errors would be made for things that others 'in the know' had long since developed workarounds. By the time I left in 2012, technicians were kept to certain small groups of trains to reduce this problem of unfamiliarity and there was also less switching between day and night working.

Working the NMT

You know how it is; you look back on something through those rose-tinted spectacles and say something was the best. Well, I'll not break with tradition: My time onboard the New Measurement Train *was* the best job I ever had. OK, there were many early mornings and late nights when I'd wonder what I'd let myself in for … and times when I just wanted to get home and catch up on lost sleep! But I do look back on it all with pride and a feeling that those of us who developed and operated the NMT (and indeed the other trains in the monitoring fleet) helped to make the railways significantly safer than they'd been before.

So how was the NMT operated? All the OTTs were split into four teams of three, originally with the intention that one of the three would act as the train's guard. It was then decided that it would be better to treat it as a driver-only-operated train, thus passing more responsibility on to the driver for the purposes of route knowledge and overall

No. 43067 enjoys the sunshine at Etches Park alongside 43055. Cameras were never fitted to 43067/154/196 due to the short-term nature of their use on the NMT. 2 August 2005.

No. 43013 pauses in platform 6 at Crewe leading 1Z93 1551 Crewe–Longsight (via London), having been to Glasgow that morning (on my shift) and Euston that evening. 8 October 2003.

safety. One OTT acted as lead, primarily to assist the driver with safe despatch of the train from depots and stations, as well as to look after the many visitors that came onboard from time to time. OTTs were not only given PTS (track safety) training, they were also required to act as Designated Person (DP) in the event that the train was carrying non-PTS trained visitors who needed to leave the train away from a platform. This was mainly for emergencies, though there were instances where the train was unexpectedly given a non-platform road at a station where visitors were due to leave the train. The other two in the team operated the track recording equipment in the Production Vehicle PV (977994) and the Development Vehicle DV (977993); initially the train had been formed around Track Recording Coach TRC (999550) and Track Lab (977974) before the two aforementioned Mark 3 coaches became ready. It was the presence of PV and DV in the set that gave rise to the name 'New Measurement Train' – trialling and using new monitoring technologies. There are often grumbles that the train can't be considered 'new'! Having a team of three offered some flexibility because if this number was short for any reason then two people could still operate PV only. In practice, if a large number or very important group of visitors came onboard then the NMT operations manager (Eddy Locke or later, Richard Wilkinson-Ford) would likely spend a day out of their Derby office to assist. At first, the train was maintained by Maintrain at Etches Park and this proved very convenient for the train crews and technical support staff at the RTC, who only had to walk down Deadmans Lane to reach it. However it was soon transferred to Craigentinny and eventually to Heaton (where it still returns to at weekends at the time of writing).

For the NMT and the other monitoring trains, drivers and OTTs were both employed by Serco Railtest when I joined, sharing an office in Derwent House at the RTC. However, when Network Rail decided to bring the maintenance functions in-house in 2004, the OTTs switched to NR and were based in Trent House. Good relations between drivers and OTTs more or less endured, I'm pleased to say, though at the time some were doubtful of that. Some years later, the operation of the IM fleet was taken on by DB Schenker, to which the drivers then transferred in their own pool, although I noticed that enthusiasts kept referring to the 'Serco' trains for some time after!

A fortnightly roster of routes was drawn up when the NMT first started, before it was decided that the main routes needn't be covered quite so frequently and a selection of secondary lines came on to the list, once a thirteen-week cycle was introduced. The least-important lines might only be visited once in that time, whilst the WCML fast lines for instance would be covered at least three times. Week 13 was a maintenance week. One feature of the roster that didn't change (and still hasn't) is that the NMT didn't routinely run in East Anglia or on the electrified third rail network in the South. A clearance issue on the approaches to Liverpool Street has always precluded a visit using Class 43s.

On 10 April 2006 I am stood on the footbridge connecting Doncaster station with the Works as 43014 leads NMT into the West Yard there (43013 at the rear). This move allowed plenty of time for a crew change. Having travelled out from home to meet the train here, the late shift would have time to settle and have a bite to eat while the train went to Skellow Junction to reverse. Then it would record back through the station at speed and on to Kings Cross. We did the out and back run to Grantham later that night, finishing in London.

Even when the set was based away from Derby, it was important for the NMT to spend time at the RTC on a regular basis for maintenance of the monitoring kit to take place and for the replenishment of consumables. Large quantities of drinking water were consumed, so any time that it was drawn up to the apron of the EDU was an opportunity to put in an order for packs of large water bottles from the stores, stack them on to a trolley and get them onboard. There was one occasion when we knew the train was short of water but it was parked at Way & Works sidings (close to the signal box) with no prospect of moving from there before going out into service. I had a loaded trolley in tow and wasn't relishing the prospect of tugging it across the ballast, when the driver of the yard jocko 08417 spotted me and made a suggestion: we put the packs of bottles into the cab, drove it down to the sidings alongside the NMT and passed them across through an open door. Sorted! As far as the yard staff were concerned, having the NMT on site led to a significant reduction in the amount of siding space available. Ideally, it would only pay a visit during the week at a time when other train sets like the UTUs were elsewhere in the country.

When the OTTs needed to travel to and from depots or points of shift change, we would write out our own travel warrants to purchase tickets. We did quite a lot of travelling to and from departure points and shift changes. Overnight stops at hotels in London, Crewe, Manchester or Preston were common and when the train became based at Heaton, Newcastle was a frequent stopover, together with Edinburgh, too. I could almost write another book about our experiences of the hotels we stayed at and some of the taxi rides we 'enjoyed' to get to and from them! An early example of how frustrating waiting for a taxi could be at the end of a long shift happened at Ferme Park. We had booked one and were assured it would be along soon to collect us from outside Hornsey station. It was about two o'clock in the morning so we were aware of an unmarked Volvo estate pulling up shortly afterwards on the opposite side of the road, though a little distance away from the station. As we were the only people around at that time and clearly waiting on the pavement with our bags, we assumed that this wasn't our taxi but after nearly half an hour and another assurance from the taxi firm that the car should be there, we walked over to the Volvo to check. The driver said he was collecting someone from the BBC. So there was more waiting and then another call to the taxi firm to say we still hadn't been picked up. We asked what car we should be expecting … you guessed it, a Volvo! We all trooped back across the road to find out that he'd finally been told that it was railway staff he was supposed to be picking up. His excuse was that on that particular road he normally 'did a BBC job'.

Obtaining rooms in London of a reasonable standard (and within budget) could prove difficult sometimes, particularly if it was high season for the tourists or if there was a major event in the capital. But the office staff in Derby did their best for us. Certain hotels were OK if your room wasn't facing a busy thoroughfare – central London is active 24/7, after all. When you were checking in late at night, few things could be more irritating after a long shift than to find your room had been reallocated to someone else, especially when you'd gone to the trouble of ringing up earlier that evening to say you'd be arriving late, as happened to me once! OK, so they'd find a room for you in another hotel nearby but it wasn't of the same standard,

Below: Judging by the fact that my two colleagues, Dave Smith and Mike New, are stood by while I take this photo, I suspect we've got to Craigentinny to find that the train has a problem and the depot staff are still working to fix it. The exhaust from 43062, though, suggests that the start-up button has just been pressed and we'll be on our way soon. It was inside this shed that we came close to experiencing a fire on one of the generators, prevented by yours truly pressing the engine stop in the nick of time. 11 April 2005.

Overleaf: Heading a 1Z25 1436 Derby–Barrow Hill–Derby calibration run, 43013 sweeps through Duffield on a fine spring afternoon. Track Recording Coach 999550 is second in the rake but would soon be removed from the NMT, once Production Vehicle 977994 had proved itself. It is clear that this used to be a four-track section – just to the south of here the technical department of BR laid a stretch of experimental slab track during the early 1970s. 5 April 2006.

This scene was only going to occur once! The Hornby-liveried power car 43087 just happened to be stabled in Bristol Temple Meads station one Friday afternoon (ready to work a special the following day) when we were due to make a reversal in the up through road. Luckily our friendly driver Andy Parker agreed to join me on the platform to take a few shots before we were due to set off back to Paddington. 4 August 2006.

of course. As for the sort of food I enjoyed, the nasi goreng rice served at a hotel on Western Avenue was particularly good, I recall (I feel hungry just thinking about that one); likewise the fillet steak and chips (plus starter and sweet!) at the Fairfield House Hotel in Ayr – just how did I manage to get that in under my allowance?

The NMT was often called upon to undertake extra recording work in addition to its normal schedule. I took it up to Broadholme loop (south of Ambergate) one morning for the benefit of a film crew on the Network Rail helicopter (registration G-NTWK). We had special permission to run the train back and forth in the down loop for them to obtain some sequences of the train in open countryside. I received calls from the helicopter on my mobile phone and passed on instructions to the driver when they wanted us to move. Visits to the Old Dalby test track were made several times to perfect the OHL monitoring system and a requirement to obtain six foot gauging data for the future introduction of the Intercity Express Train (IET) on to the network saw us visiting a number of new places; I'm not sure if the NMT has been to Portsmouth Harbour or London Waterloo again since 19 March 2009. Or indeed to the Rylstone branch, which was my last trip on it as a fleet engineer in 2015! Of course, I always enjoyed it when we went up to Aberdeen, over the Settle and Carlisle or down to Plymouth, as these

were amongst the more scenic journeys that we made. For a time, a contract was in place for us to monitor High Speed 1 and this involved a pure night shift, the teams joining the train late evening at Kentish Town. That doesn't sound like very much work; however there were long spells of waiting involved while permission was obtained to use the link to and from HS1 and then get clearance to run at a steady 60mph to Dollands Moor and back. The train was restricted to that speed by HS1 rules. I never did manage to find the best kilometre posts for starting or finishing those runs, though!

Not long after the switch to Craigentinny for maintenance of the NMT's rolling stock (rather than the actual monitoring equipment), we realised that we were going to encounter similar difficulties to what we had before. My notes from 22 November 2004 stated (on my team's arrival there one Monday): 'A taxi takes us from Waverley to the depot where we find the staff still working to sort out problems which should have been attended to over the weekend – shades of Etches Park, we're clearly not at the top of their list of priorities. One of their fitters starts generator 1 in 975984 and takes power from it, only for me to have to investigate why it's sounding very rough and issuing smoke from places that it shouldn't. I shut it down and the generator room immediately fills with smoky steam. Making a sharp exit, I catch sight of a worried-looking fitter outside who asks me whether it's on fire. I suspect not (and thankfully it isn't!) but that's one generator we aren't going to be using anytime soon. I later find out that the radiator was practically dry and that if I hadn't shut the engine down when I did, it might well have been a write-off. We revert to generator 2 in 977984. Optel (the laser system) plays up as we run an hour late into Waverley station to begin recording. Unusually we get bay platform 7, which at least means we can inspect underneath without needing to get a block on any adjacent lines. The skirting next to the laser seems damaged but eventually the system finds both rails and we are off. Only 45 minutes down at the Doncaster shift changeover – could have been worse.

'On the following Saturday, I'm working the train back to Edinburgh. The driver gets a shock soon after we leave Derby when he has a green signal off the down goods line near Breadsall, only to get a red at the next one on the main. Having been accelerating on full power, he passes it by about 100 yards. A few minutes discussion with the box on the cab phone ensues (the red was caused by a defective button on the box panel) and we are away again, only for him to see a big black cow walking into the four foot ahead. More emergency braking!

'Control calls me to ensure that the driver's OK to continue. All in a day's work …?'

One very typical shift that we did in the early years of running was the one mid-Tuesday afternoon that began at the RTC, covering the slow lines of the WCML south from Lichfield and finishing at Manchester Piccadilly sometime after midnight. The train would be 'prepped' in the yard first, one of the team drawing the short straw and giving the camera pods underneath PV a clean by lying on a rubber mat next to the bogie and reaching underneath with a cloth – not pleasant in the wet or the cold! The other would start the generator and power up the computers in PV and DV, creating files to which the data would get written and check for any emails sent to inform us of last-minute requests or changes. All being well, the kettle would go on for the driver to receive his first brew of the shift after he'd carried out his own checks, at which point the routing would be discussed and notification of possible visitors given (in case a special stop was required to pick them up or drop them off). We'd then draw up to the station to make a reversal on the goods lines before making a transit move to Lichfield Trent Valley, via the high- to low-level curve. Actual recording southwards would start at milepost 116 and finish approaching the Euston throat. Following a stopping service for much of our final 50 miles into the capital, the driver had to regulate his speed so as not to have to stop at a red signal, because dropping below 10–15mph meant losing recording data. He would almost always have to phone the signaller to get us the correct line in from Camden, as this never seemed to get put into the timings. A break of around three-quarters of an hour would be taken at Euston. This gave us a chance to stretch our legs or buy some food to eat during the slow journey north.

No. 43062 rests inside the shed at Old Oak Common HST depot after arriving from Derby, via Bristol. 16 March 2007.

Passing the time, I remember once being told by a member of station staff there that I couldn't take a photo of my own train! There's always one …

Late-evening possessions in the Crewe area would often lead to us being put 'off route' in places or diverted via Styal or Winwick Junction on the way to Piccadilly. The aim then was to burn the data on to DVDs quickly (for return to the office next day) so that we could shut down the equipment and leave the train in the platform there; otherwise, we'd need to stay onboard while the train went off to stable at Longsight depot and have to call for a taxi to take us back into central Manchester to our hotel. Red faces were in order when a team detrained at Manchester Oxford Road in the early hours (having finished their recording before passing Winwick Junction) with a view to getting quickly to their nearby hotel; it was a good idea, only the station was locked up and they couldn't get out! With the NMT disappearing off towards Longsight, they were rescued by another passing train, which took them to Piccadilly.

Timely communication with other teams and Control proved important. One time when that didn't happen, we arrived at Longsight on the Wednesday morning to find the train hadn't got there the previous night and was still at Crewe. I think we managed to call back the same taxi

driver who had just dropped us off. Another time, our service train from Derby to Cheltenham (where we were due to relieve another team) was delayed and by the time we arrived, the other team and the NMT had gone. Gone where? Not Alstone carriage siding (an FGW HST was occupying that) but the far end of Lansdown loop, nearly a mile's walk away down the side of the track – not much fun on a hot summer's afternoon with heavy bags to carry. A more pleasant memory from the west of England though was eating hot pasties from the station shop at Plymouth after we'd made the early start from Old Oak Common. When you'd not had much sleep in your central London hotel room the previous night and only a croissant for breakfast, those pasties were a godsend!

Traction and rolling stock troubles beset the train many times during its first two years of operation and I have written an article about that for *Rail Express* magazine (September 2018 issue). The three power cars that became available for use with the train in 2003 (43013/14/62) became available for a reason – they were in serious need of an overhaul. They looked nice enough in their new yellow livery but when the throttle was opened the resultant exhaust showed that their power units were in as poor a state as any Paxman Valentas were in the country. Several complete failures out on the line

Recently modified with new headlight clusters, 43062 has arrived at Hull (in company with 43089) and the NMT will shortly be on its way back to Derby and then Crewe for an overnight stop. Jason Rogers is conducting Colin Campbell on this occasion. Drivers' shifts didn't always coincide with those of the OTTs, especially with the NMT as it could cover long distances in the working day. TRU, however, might utilise the same driver over several days and staying in the same hotels as the train team, particularly in Wales and Scotland. 22 April 2008.

EMT meets NMT? Power car 43013 is seen at Leeds Neville Hill depot in the company of EMT shunter 08950 and East Coast Trains 43314. During the Saturday shift when the NMT ran from Derby to Heaton, via the Settle and Carlisle, it would wait here for a spell before taking up its path northwards to Carlisle. 28 May 2011.

didn't endear Network Rail to the train operators so, at the first opportunity, a further power car (43154) was hired to relieve the pressure on the other three. With another promised (43067), the original three were released one by one for reliability modifications to be made by DML at Devonport (re-engining with MTU power units at Brush came later). In early 2006, a third hired power car (43196) came on the scene for us and 43067/154 went off to join Grand Central and FGW respectively.

That year on 1 February, during a recording of the up slow into Euston, we were stopped and told to inspect the train following reports of sparks coming from underneath. The powerful lighting from the Cybernetix system on DV shone vertically down on to the ballast, tending to cause reflections in a flickering manner, so we already had a good idea what the cause was. What we didn't know was that having to take a block on the adjacent lines to make our inspection was delaying a Pendolino behind us … carrying half the Network Rail board! The serving Head of Innovation and Examination, Gary Sanford was with them and no doubt getting a bit of flak; whether that incident had anything to do with his taking early retirement some months later, I've no idea but I wouldn't have blamed him. They were stressful times.

Hot weather that August proved over-taxing for the air conditioning in the train, all reminiscent of when the NMT project started in 2003 when we had a long and hot summer to enjoy. Then on the way back to Derby from Bristol one Friday afternoon, the Laserail system began playing up and producing all kinds of spurious readings. Rather than stop specially (and cause delays) we waited for the train to sight a red signal and got the driver's permission to make a very quick inspection underneath while he waited. Would you believe that a damp copy of the *Metro* free newspaper was wrapped around a camera? And don't they just love to run stories knocking the railways?

From May 2007 (and with the NMT's power cars running much more reliably now), the train began to widen its sphere of operations. On 16 October, we ran from Derby to Hull on this circuitous route: Derby–Sheffield–Doncaster–Hull–Joan Croft Jn–Bentley Jn–Hexthorpe Jn–Swinton–Aldwarke Jn–Rotherham Central–Woodburn Jn–Gainsborough Trent Jn–Shireoaks East Jn–Shirebrook–Pye Bridge Jn–Trowell Jn–Lenton South Jn–Trent Jn–Derby.

Sunderland, Holyhead, Aberdeen, the S&C, Trans-Pennine and Marches routes began to be visited by the NMT now that its new track recording system had been signed off and the frequency of covering certain main routes reduced.

NMT sits in the south bay at York, having come from Newcastle via the Settle and Carlisle route. My shift on it began at Leeds and we are now working across to Manchester, en route to Derby. Our driver, Jason Rogers, in 43062 observes a Grand Central HST, headed by 43423 leaving for Kings Cross past East Coast DVT 82217. 25 April 2011.

A typical two weeks of operation follows:

		RST No.	Miles
MONDAY, 21 MAY 2007			
Shift 1	**Timed to start around 1045hrs.**		
Transit	Heaton Depot – Newcastle Station (RM)		
Record	Newcastle–Down Main–Morpeth–Alnmouth–Berwick– Dunbar–Drem–Prestonpans–Monktonhall Jn–Edinburgh	048/1 pt	124
WTT 1Z22: Edinburgh 1249 hrs–Glasgow–Newcastle 1729 hrs.			
Record	Edinburgh–Down South Line–Haymarket–Down South– Down E & G–Newbridge Jn–Down Main–Polmont–Falkirk High– Down Main–Glasgow Queen Street (RM)	035/2	47
Record	Glasgow Queen Street–Up Main–Falkirk High–Polmont– Up Main–Newbridge Jn–Up E & G–Up South Line–Haymarket–Up South–Edinburgh	035/1	47
Record	Edinburgh–Monktonhall Jn–Prestonpans–Drem–Dunbar– Berwick–Alnmouth–Morpeth–Up Main–Newcastle Platform 3 (C/S)	048/2 pt	124
Shift 2			
Record	Newcastle–Durham–Darlington–Northallerton–York–Colton Jn– Up Main–Doncaster–Swinton Jn–Masborough Jn–Sheffield– Dronfield–Chesterfield–Ambergate Jn–Derby Station–Derby RTC Stable at Derby RTC	048/2 pt 019/1	113 55

TUESDAY, 22 MAY 2007	**RST No.**	**Miles**

WTT 1Z95: Derby 1503 hrs–Euston–Crewe 2203 hrs.

Transit	Derby RTC–Derby Station (RM)–Stenson Jn–Burton–Wichnor Jn– Lichfield TV Curve–Lichfield Dn & Up GL (RM)		
Record	Lichfield Trent Valley–Tamworth–Up Slow–Nuneaton–Up Slow– Rugby Platform 2–Up Northampton–Hanslope Jn–Up Slow–Bletchley– Up Slow–Camden Jn–Line B–London Euston Platform 7 (Traincrew personal needs break (PNB) (RM)	016/2 pt	113
Record	London Euston–Line C–Camden Jn–Down Slow–Bletchley– Down Slow–Hanslope Jn–Down Northampton–Rugby Platform 1– Brinklow DPL–Attleborough Jn–Down Slow–Nuneaton–Down Slow– Tamworth–Lichfield Trent Valley–Down Slow–Armitage Jn–Down Slow– Colwich Jn–Milford Jn–Down Slow– Stafford–Down Slow–Norton Bridge– Down Slow–Madeley–Down Slow–Crewe (RM)	016/1 pt	134
Record	Crewe–Up Slow–Madeley–Up Slow–Norton Bridge–Up Slow– Stafford–Up Slow–Colwich Jn–Up Slow–Lichfield Up Slow	016/2 pt	33
Transit	Lichfield TV Curve–Wichnor Jn–Burton–Stenson Jn–Derby Station (RM)– Derby RTC Refuel and stable at Derby RTC		

John Gorman has got hold of my camera and captured three OTTs clearly hard at work in NMT's Production Vehicle ... well, one is anyway. John Bradley is looking at the log while Karl Garlick and me look a bit silly. I avoided wearing orange trousers! The train is somewhere in the Birmingham area, having gone to Stockport that morning with the extra crew member to operate the overhead and pantograph monitoring system. 12 May 2011.

It seems I have the job of going underneath the NMT at Heaton to clean the cameras. It looks straightforward enough but unless you are short, it's not easy having to walk the length of four vehicles while bent double! The train featured in a depot open day here on 14 September 2008. 9 May 2011.

WEDNESDAY, 25 MAY 2007

Instrumentation Maintenance at RTC

THURSDAY, 24 MAY 2007		**RST No.**	**Miles**

Shift 1
WTT 1Z94: Derby 0730–St Pancras–Derby 1456 hrs.

Transit	Derby RTC–Derby Station (RM)		
Record	Derby–Spondon–Sheet Stores Jn–Trent South Jn–Up Fast– Loughborough–Up Fast–Leicester–Market Harborough–Kettering– Up Fast–Wellingborough–Up Fast–Bedford–Up Fast–Luton–Up Fast– London St Pancras (RM)	063/2	128
Record	London St Pancras–U&D Slow–Carlton Road–Down Slow– Luton–Down Slow–Bedford (RM)	063/4	50
Record	Bedford–Up Slow–Luton–Up Slow–Carlton Road Jn– Up & Dn Relief–London St Pancras (RM)	063/5	50
Record	London St Pancras–Down Fast–Luton–Down Fast–Bedford– Down Fast–Wellingborough–Down Fast–Kettering–Market Harborough– Leicester–Down Fast–Loughborough–Down Fast–Trent South Jn– Sheet Stores Jn–Spondon–Derby Station (RM)	063/1	128
Transit	Derby Station–Derby RTC. Stable at Derby RTC		

I was aware of the intention to close the signal box at Yeovil Junction so having worked the NMT on the morning shift to Exeter, I stayed onboard back to there and walked up the track to be in position for this photo. Steve Sheehan is in the cab of 43013 and the working was 1Q23 0446 Old Oak Common–Salisbury (via Exeter). 22 September 2011.

Shift 2

WTT 1Z98: Derby 1640 hrs–Bristol 1930 hrs.

		RST No.	Miles
Transit	Derby RTC–Derby Station (RM)		
Record	Derby–Down Main West/Down Main–Stenson Jn–Burton– Down Main–Wichnor Jn–Tamworth–Kingsbury Jn–Down Fast–Water Orton– Down Main–Landor St Jn–Down Camp Hill–Kings Norton–Down Fast– Barnt Green–Bromsgrove– Stoke Works Jn–Abbotswood Jn–Cheltenham Spa– Barnwood Jn–Down Avoiding–Gloucester Yard Jn–Standish Jn– Westerleigh Jn–Bristol Parkway–Down Main–Bristol Temple Meads (Traincrew PNB)	834/2	126
Record	Bristol Temple Meads (Down Thro)–Down Main–Worle Jn– Uphill Jn–Bridgwater–Cogload Jn	002/1 pt	40
Transit	Cogload Jn–Taunton (RM)–Cogload Jn		
Record	Cogload Jn–Bridgwater–Uphill Jn–Worle Jn–Up Main– Bristol Temple Meads Platform 7–Bath Spa–Wootton Bassett Jn– Swindon (RM)	002/2	76
Record	Swindon–Bath Spa–Bristol Temple Meads (Down Thro) (RM)	002/1 pt	36
Record	Bristol Temple Meads–Up Filton Main–Bristol Parkway	834/1 pt	6
Record	Bristol Parkway–Swindon–Up Main–Didcot Parkway–Up Main– Reading–Up Main–Line 3–London Paddington (RM)	001/2 pt	112
Transit	London Paddington–Old Oak Common Refuel and stable at Old Oak Common		

With work on the station roof in progress, One Quebec Zero Eight is in platform 7 at Kings Cross and will soon depart for Leeds. When we started doing this run in 2003, the NMT would stable at Bounds Green overnight and work this leg early in the morning. 17 October 2011.

FRIDAY, 25 MAY 2007		RST No.	Miles

WTT 5C00: Old Oak Common 0551 hrs–Paddington 0606 hrs.
WTT 1C00: Paddington 0619 hrs as far as Swindon 0713 hrs.

Transit	Old Oak Common–London Paddington (RM)		
Record	London Paddington–Line 2–Down Main–Reading–Down Main– Swindon–Bristol Parkway–Down Main–Newport Platform 2–Down Main– Cardiff–Down Main–Swansea (RM) (Traincrew PNB)	001/1	190
Record	Swansea–Up Main–Cardiff–Up Main–Newport Platform 3– Up Main–Bristol Parkway (C/S)	001/2 pt	80
Record	Bristol Parkway–Westerleigh Jn–Standish Jn–Gloucester Yard Jn– Up Avoiding–Barnwood Jn–Cheltenham Spa–Abbotswood Jn– Stoke Works Jn–Bromsgrove– Barnt Green–Up Fast–Kings Norton– Up Camp Hill–Landor St Jn–Up Main–Water Orton–Up Fast–Tamworth– Wichnor Jn–Burton–Up Main–Stenson Jn–Up Main–Derby Station (RM)	834/1	126
Transit	Derby Station–Derby RTC. Stable at Derby RTC		

SATURDAY, 26 MAY 2007

WTT 1Z19: Derby 0850 hrs–Newcastle 1221 hrs.

Transit	Derby RTC–Derby Station–Ambergate Jn–Chesterfield–Dronfield–Sheffield– Masborough Jn–Swinton Jn–Doncaster–Down Main–Colton Jn–York– Northallerton– Darlington–Durham–Newcastle–Heaton Depot Refuel, Stable and Maintenance at Heaton Depot

		RST No.	Miles
TUESDAY, 29 MAY 2007			

<u>Shift 1</u>   **Timed to start 1045 hrs.**

Transit   Heaton Depot–Newcastle

Record   Newcastle–Up Main/Up Fast–Durham–Up Fast–Darlington–   **048/2 pt**   **269**
Up Main–Northallerton–Up Fast–York Platform 3–Up Main–Colton Jn–
Up Main–Doncaster–Up Fast–Retford–Up Main–Newark Northgate–
Up Main–Grantham–Up Fast–Peterborough–Up Fast– Kings Cross (RM)

Transit   Kings Cross–Ferme Park
Refuel – Allow 1 hour

Transit   Ferme Park–Bowes Park Jn (RM)–Bounds Green

<u>Shift 2</u>   **Timed to start 1845 hrs.**

Transit   Bounds Green–Kings Cross (RM)

Record   Kings Cross–Down Fast–Peterborough–Down Fast–Grantham–   **048/6**   **185**
Down Main–Newark Northgate–Down Main–Retford–Down Main/Down Fast–
Doncaster Down Fast–Marshgate Jn–South Kirkby Jn–Hare Park Jn–
Wakefield Westgate–Copley Hill East Jn–Line 'C'–Leeds (RM)

Record   Leeds–Line 'D'–Copley Hill East Jn–Wakefield Westgate–   **048/9**   **29**
Hare Park Jn–South Kirkby Jn–Marshgate Jn–Doncaster
(Traincrew PNB)

Record   Doncaster–Swinton Jn–Masborough Jn–Sheffield Platform 6–   **019/2**   **55**
Dronfield–Chesterfield–Ambergate Jn–Up Main–Derby Station–Derby RTC
Stable at Derby RTC

		RST No.	Miles
WEDNESDAY, 30 MAY 2007			

<u>Shift 1</u>   **Timed to start 0530 hrs.**

Transit   Derby RTC–Derby Station (RM)–Stenson Jn–Uttoxeter–Stoke–Kidsgrove–
Alsager– Crewe (C/S)

WTT 1Z92: Crewe 0651 hrs–Glasgow–Crewe 1501 hrs.

Record   Crewe–Down Fast–Weaver Jn–Acton Grange Jn–Down Main–   **015/1 pt**   **243**
Warrington Bank Quay–Down Fast–Winwick Jn–Golborne Jn–Down Fast–
Wigan NW–Balshaw Lane Jn–Down Fast–Euxton Jn–Down Fast–
Preston Platform 3–Down Main–Lancaster–Carnforth–Oxenholme–
Shap Summit–Penrith–Carlisle (C/S)–Down Main–Gretna Jn–Lockerbie–
Carstairs–Motherwell–Rutherglen East Jn–Down Fast–Glasgow Central (RM)

Record   Glasgow Central–Up Fast–Rutherglen East Jn–Motherwell–   **015/2 pt**   **243**
Carstairs–Lockerbie–Gretna Jn–Up Main–Carlisle (C/S)–Penrith–Shap Summit–
Oxenholme– Carnforth–Lancaster–Preston Platform 4–Up Fast–Euxton Jn–
Balshaw Lane Jn–Wigan NW– Up Fast–Golborne Jn–Winwick Jn–Up Fast–
Warrington Bank Quay–Up Main–Acton Grange Jn–Weaver Jn–Up Fast–Crewe

Transit   Crewe Station–LNWR. Refuel at Crewe LNWR

<u>Shift 2</u>

Transit   Crewe LNWR–Crewe Station (RM)

WTT 1Z93: Crewe 1640 hrs–Euston–Crewe–Derby 2343 hrs.

Record   Crewe–Up Fast–Madeley–Up Fast–Norton Bridge–Up Fast–   **014/9**   **158**
Stafford–Up Fast–Colwich Jn–Up Fast–Lichfield Trent Valley–Up Fast–
Tamworth–Up Fast– Nuneaton–Up Fast–Rugby–Up Main (via Weedon)–
Hanslope Jn–Up Fast–Bletchley– Up Fast–Watford Jn–Up Fast–Camden Jn–
Line D–London Euston Middle Sdg (RM)
(Traincrew PNB)

		RST No.	Miles
Record	London Euston–Line E–Camden Jn–Down Fast– Watford Jn–Down Fast–Bletchley–Down Fast–Hanslope Jn–Down Main (via Weedon)–Rugby–Down Fast–Nuneaton–Down Fast–Tamworth–Lichfield– Down Fast–Colwich Jn– Down Fast–Stafford–Down Fast–Norton Bridge– Down Fast–Madeley–Down Fast–Crewe (RM)	014/8	158
Transit	Crewe–Madeley–Norton Bridge–Stafford–Colwich Jn–Lichfield TV Curve– Alrewas– Wichnor Jn–Burton–Stenson Jn–Derby Station (RM)–Derby RTC Refuel and stable at Derby RTC		

THURSDAY, 31 MAY 2007

		RST No.	Miles
Shift 1	**Timed to start 0800 hrs.**		
Transit	Derby RTC–Derby Station (RM)–Stenson Jn–Burton–Wichnor Jn–Tamworth– Water Orton–Landor St Jn–Birmingham New Street–Galton Jn		
Record	Galton Jn–Rowley Regis–Stourbridge Jn–Kidderminster– Droitwich Spa–Worcester Shrub Hill (RM)	807/2	31
Record	Worcester Shrub Hill–Great Malvern–Hereford (RM)	011/1	28
Record	Hereford–Great Malvern–Worcester Shrub Hill (Traincrew PNB)	011/2	11
Transit	Worcester Shrub Hill–Norton Jn–Abbotswood Jn–Cheltenham Spa– Barnwood Jn– Down Avoiding–Gloucester Yard Jn–Standish Jn		
Record	Standish Jn–Stroud–Kemble–Swindon (RM)	010/2	17
Record	Swindon–Kemble–Stroud–Standish Jn	010/1	29
Transit	Standish Jn–Gloucester Yard Jn–Up Avoiding–Barnwood Jn–Cheltenham Spa– Alstone Carriage Sdgs (RM)		
Shift 2	**Timed to start following end of shift 1.**		
Transit	Alstone Carriage Sdgs–Cheltenham Spa–Barnwood Jn		
Record	Barnwood Jn–Down Main–Gloucester Platform 1/2–Lydney– Chepstow–Severn Tunnel Jn	009/1	36
Record	Severn Tunnel Jn–Down Relief–Newport–Down Relief– Cardiff Central Platform 7	001/6	21
Record	Cardiff Central–Penarth Curve South–Cogan Jn–Barry–Aberthaw– Bridgend (RM)	801/1	27
Record	Bridgend–Aberthaw–Barry–Cogan Jn–Penarth Curve South Jn– Cardiff Central Platform 6	801/2	27
Record	Cardiff Central–Up Relief–Newport–Up Relief–Severn Tunnel Jn	001/7	21
Record	Severn Tunnel Jn–Chepstow–Lydney–Gloucester Up Main – Barnwood Jn	009/2	36
Transit	Barnwood Jn–Cheltenham Spa–Abbotswood Jn–Norton Jn–Worcester Shrub Hill		
Record	Worcester Shrub Hill–Droitwich Spa–Kidderminster– Stourbridge Jn–Rowley Regis–Galton Jn	807/1	31
Transit	Galton Jn–Birmingham New Street–Landor St Jn–Water Orton–Tamworth– Wichnor Jn–Burton–Stenson Jn–Derby Station (RM)–Derby RTC		

FRIDAY, 1 JUNE 2007

Instrumentation Maintenance at RTC

I suppose this was a bit naughty but after a very quick glance out of the window to check no train was approaching us, I've held the camera out at arm's length from the generator vehicle and fired the shutter a few times to obtain one good shot. I would have been lead OTT at the time, so wouldn't have been required to operate any recording equipment at that particular moment! No. 43062 is heading the NMT southward across the Forth Bridge on return from Inverkeithing. This extra piece of recording, simply over the bridge and back to Edinburgh (on the end of a Derby–Craigentinny shift), came about in response to a TV programme that had claimed the track on the bridge wasn't being maintained properly. 23 November 2010.

SATURDAY, 2 JUNE 2007   RST No.   Miles

WTT 1Z19: Derby 0850 hrs–Newcastle 1221 hrs.

Transit	Derby RTC–Derby Station		
Record	Derby Station–Down Main–Ambergate Jn–Chesterfield–Dronfield–Sheffield Platform 2–Masborough Jn–Swinton Jn–Doncaster	019/1	55
Record	Doncaster Down Fast/Down Main–Colton Jn–Down Main–York Platform 5–Down Fast–Northallerton–Darlington–Down Main–Durham–Newcastle	048/1 pt	113
Transit	Newcastle–Morpeth–Alnmouth–Berwick–Dunbar–Drem–Prestonpans–Edinburgh (RM)–Craigentinny Depot Power Car Swap–Allow one hour		
Transit	Craigentinny Depot–Edinburgh (RM)–Prestonpans–Drem–Dunbar–Berwick–Alnmouth–Morpeth–Heaton Depot Refuel, Stable and Maintenance at Heaton Depot.		

In the cab of 43062, driver George Jones concentrates on the road ahead as the NMT cruises at 110mph along the up fast through Cheddington, south of Leighton Buzzard. All seems fine, but look closely and you will see something amiss at the fourth coach – a flapping equipment hatch on the skirting. I contacted our Control immediately to find out who was on shift and then called them. The train was stopped, the hatch secured and then checked again when they reached Euston. This was just as well as on their northbound return run it could quite easily have struck a platform edge and gone flying in any direction. 26 January 2010.

NMT Visitors

When plans for the NMT were drawn up, it was decided that the opportunity would be taken to create a train that would also serve as a bit of a flagship for Network Rail. Up to that time, the only types of special train available for use by senior management were inspection saloons and these weren't capable of high-speed running. One of the NMT's Mark 3s (975814) was therefore equipped as a conference coach with a long table and a dozen comfortable seats in front of a video screen for presentations, the idea being that it could be used for team meetings away from the office; and not only for the company's directors. It also had a small separate office and semicircular bench seating area so that more than one group could be entertained simultaneously. In the middle was a messing area from which refreshments could be distributed; in the event, only teas and coffees tended to be prepared here and any food was usually brought onboard on the day. Provided that this coach was available, any group of staff in the company could in theory join it at a suitable location to hold their meeting and then (more importantly) take the opportunity to walk through to view the monitoring work going on in the other coaches.

In plain all-over yellow, 43062 *John Armitt* heads NMT through Kentish Town on the slow lines circuit back from Bedford to St Pancras. The train has six coaches in the rake, as 977995 has been included and one of the regular generator coaches hasn't been removed. I'm in London ready to work EMV (with top and tail 73s) from Bramdean Sidings early the following morning. 29 September 2011.

Right: Looking down on to the roof equipment bay of NMT Development Vehicle 977993 at Evesham. The motion of the pantograph and the behaviour of the Fraunhofer contactless measuring system could be observed on a monitor down below, via the cameras mounted in the small windows at each end of the bay. A band of light was shone upwards from the box marked with the yellow 'Danger' sign and the Fraunhofer system would use its own cameras to measure the position and condition of the overhead wire; this would operate independently of the pantograph, though would complement any contact data acquired if the pan was raised. The idea was that this arrangement would supplant the operation of 'Mentor' on the main electrified routes, at least. However, in something of a 'chicken and egg' situation, use of the pantograph on DV could not be fully signed off for regular use as no other such Mark 3 coach had ever worked with a pantograph in this way, so there was little historic data to support the case. That was my interpretation of it, anyway – others might provide a different story. The Fraunhofer contactless system became fully operational, though. 15 July 2010.

Below: The screen in NMT's Development Vehicle (977993) displaying information on height and stagger of the overhead wire. The horizontal lines represent stanchions and I believe the group of three close together are showing a neutral section. The OTTs just had to make sure that this system was running satisfactorily; no fault reporting on wire issues from the train took place, except if the wires had actually come down, of course!

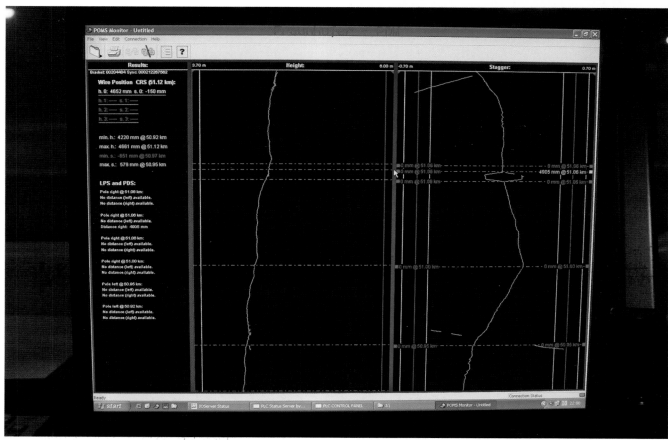

Inside the cab of 43062. This loco suffered from vibration stemming from derailment damage and was said to be the reason why it had been made available for Network Rail to use on the NMT. Note the important handled item on the centre console – most messages from cab to train seemed to be to 'put the kettle on!'

After seeing all the visitors on to the train and issuing safety instructions to those assembled ('don't try getting off the train without my say-so', 'don't pull the red communication handles without checking with me first', 'your life vest is under your seat' etc, etc.), the lead OTT was often expected to give a short presentation about what the IM fleet did and how it contributed to the safe running of the railway. This could be a little nerve-wracking, particularly if the video equipment was playing up, as it often did. But the reward was often some nice sandwiches or biscuits (shared with the rest of the team!), so that was OK. We had to make sure they all had time to walk through to the Production and Development Vehicles in smallish groups to see what was going on and ask some questions. Shaking hands, thanking everyone for coming at the end of their visit and hearing some immediate feedback on how much they enjoyed it was certainly one of the more rewarding aspects of the job.

Interestingly, at around the same time NMT was being put together it became apparent that English, Welsh and Scottish Railways was assembling its own management train, also with Mark 3s and a video screen. But being only for the use of the EWS top brass, we regarded it as a gin palace – not really a serious working train like ours!

The popular choice for NMT visits, certainly for London-based office staff, was the Midland Mainline run where we recorded the up fast line from Derby to St Pancras (arriving around 10am), the slows out to Bedford and return, followed by the down fast line back to Derby in the afternoon. Quite often one group would travel with us from Derby and spend a couple of hours in London while a separate one came on just for the Bedford trip. I recall being the lead OTT when the then NR chairman, Ian McAllister (who used to run Ford in Britain), held a press conference onboard the NMT during the Bedford trip and he seemed very anxious to return to his office, once we had pulled into St Pancras. I had to prevent him from opening the carriage door before I'd got permission from the driver to let people off. The trip was a convenient venue for this sort of thing, not least because everyone could be back at their office in time for lunch!

A team from the Welsh Assembly were booked to join us at Swansea one morning with a view to inspecting the recently reopened platform 4 at Newport. We brought the train up from London on its usual Paddington to Swansea run to begin with and as we passed through Newport, I noticed a clutch of people wielding paintbrushes, clearly applying some last-minute finishing touches to the steelwork. I just hoped the paint would be dry by the time we came back. Hosting the Assembly team was Robbie Burns, then director of NR's Western Zone. I remember the uncomfortable look on his face when during my presentation

A view looking down the banks of racks in DV (977993). The author recalls the extreme interest shown in these during the visit by a delegation of Chinese railway engineers; pocket digital cameras were much in evidence on that occasion and clearly tolerated, in stark contrast to the experiences of enthusiasts at certain railway stations I won't mention!

I (truthfully) explained to his guests that the track recording system was good but not foolproof!

Another time, we had a delegation of officials from Chinese Railways; they seemed to want to take photographs of everything on the train, inside and out ... hmm, I wonder why? I'm not aware of a lookalike NMT running around China yet, though! I had a pleasant chat with tie-averse Richard Bowker, head of the Strategic Rail Authority, when he paid a visit. Not long after that the SRA was abolished by Transport Secretary Alistair Darling, no doubt thinking that he needed to do at least something to mark his time in office; I don't remember him coming out to see us in action. Non-railway industry figures who were also entertained on my shifts included the former Archbishop of York, Dr David Hope, and Chris Barrie, as part of the filming for a TV programme called *Massive Speed* that he was introducing for the Discovery Channel. Looking through the visitor's book, I noticed that former *Tomorrow's World* presenter Maggie Philbin had been and left some positive comments about what we did, I believe during a visit by her company Teentech, which helps youngsters get an introduction to careers in science, technology and engineering. 'All good stuff,' as John Lord in our Derby Control office was inclined to say.

When the Hitachi hybrid traction package was incorporated into the set, we got to meet some high-ranking engineers from Japan. The power car 43089 *Hayabusa* and supporting battery vehicle 977996 didn't require any input from us, the only noticeable difference being that you didn't hear the diesel engine building up revs until the train had reached around 20mph.

A large group that I didn't have the pleasure of hosting was one heading for the Conservative Party Conference at Blackpool, during a run from Euston on 29 September 2007 specially arranged on the command of Network Rail HQ (see figures B, C and D). The company was obviously keen to make a good impression on those who they felt might be in government at some point! Looking down the list of MPs, advisors and journalists, it's tempting to ask 'where are they now?' But the stand-out feature of this particular trip was that it was the only time (to the best of my knowledge) that alcohol was served aboard the NMT. And absolutely none was left over for the next shift to get a sniff of, or much food for that matter. Believe me, they checked! How did everyone fit into the conference coach, you may wonder? Well they didn't – by making full use of both messing vehicles though (another couple of dozen seats), everyone could sit down for at least part of their journey. Judging by the schedule, I'm guessing they took the slow lines for most of the way; and I don't think the train has turned left out of Preston since!

AGENDA

New Measurement Train (NMT) to the
Annual Conservative Party Conference 2007

11.20-11.30	**Guests assemble at the Virgin First Class lounge, London Euston**
11.30-12.00noon	**Passengers board the NMT:** *Luggage check in and registration*
12.00noon	**Train departs** *Canapés and welcome drinks served* *Welcome from Ian McAllister, Chairman and Iain Coucher, Chief Executive, Network Rail*
12.30	**Lunch**
Between 14.00-16.30	**A range of optional activities** *Passengers are welcome to attend a presentation, entitled "2030 Railway" in the Boardroom, a tour of the train and there will be an opportunity to meet with Network Rail representatives.*
From 15.30	**Afternoon tea served in mess cars**
17.00	**Arrival in Blackpool North**

Figure B

Passengers

- David Amess MP
- John Bowis MEP
- Angie Bray AM
- James Brokenshire MP, Shadow Home Affairs Minister
- Anthony Browne, Director of Policy Exchange
- Greg Clark MP, Shadow Minister for the Cabinet Office
- Roger Evans AM, Chair of the London Assembly Transport Committee
- Mark Francois MP, Shadow Minister for Europe
- Michael Gove MP, Shadow Secretary of State for Children, Schools and Families
- Sally Hammond
- Stephen Hammond MP, Shadow Rail Minister
- Dr Oliver Marc Hartwich, Chief Economist, Policy Exchange
- Charles Hendry MP, Shadow Minister for Trade and Industry
- Mark Hoban MP, Shadow Treasury Minister
- Elizabeth Howlett AM
- Bernard Jenkin MP
- Anne Jenkin
- Dr Robert Kinghorn, Conservative Transport Group
- Julie Kirkbride MP
- Andrew MacKay MP, Political Adviser to David Cameron
- Daisy McAndrew, Chief Political Correspondent, ITN
- Anne Milton MP, Shadow Minister for Health
- Andrew Pierce, Telegraph, Deputy Editor, The Telegraph
- Andrew Rosindell MP, Shadow Home Office Minister
- Richard Spring MP, Vice Chairman of the Conservative Party
- Theresa Villiers MP, Shadow Secretary of State for Transport
- Angela Watkinson MP, Opposition Whip
- John Whittingdale MP, Chair of Culture, Media and Sports Select Committee
- Bill Wiggin MP, Shadow Minister for Agriculture and Fisheries

Network Rail hosts

- Ian McAllister, Chairman
- Iain Coucher, Chief Executive
- Victoria Pender, Group Director, Government and Corporate Affairs
- Andrew McNaughton, Chief Engineer
- Garry White, Head of Public Affairs
- Eddy Locke, Examination Technical Specialist (Head of NMT)
- David Williams, Head of Westwood (Network Rail's Leadership Development Centre)
- Duncan Stephenson, Public Affairs Manager

Figure C

The New Measurement Train

Network Rail's New Measurement Train (NMT) plays an important role inspecting and assessing the condition of the track and other infrastructure so that engineers can plan and prioritise where to carry out maintenance works on the network.

The train measures many things including ride quality, track and overhead line alignment and radio signal strengths for critical communications systems employed on the railway network. Lasers and other instruments are used to make measurements of the track geometry and features such as overhead line height, and track gauge. The train captures video footage from the front and rear power cars, and video of the pantograph and wheel interfaces.

The NMT was launched in 2003, and was converted from extensively overhauled and modified existing vehicles released from High Speed passenger trains by the Industry. In 2005 it won an award for Innovation in Engineering at the Railway Forum/Modern Railways Innovation Awards. The formation of the train is: power car, messing car, development systems vehicle, track recording systems vehicle, meeting coach with conference area, messing car and power car.

The development systems vehicle includes a vibrating platform close to the rails, detecting missing Pandrol clips. The vehicle also houses the pantograph used to detect faults in overhead wires. White lights next to the pantograph project a line followed by cameras to enable the height and stagger of the overhead lines to be monitored. No traction or system power is drawn using the pantograph, as the train is diesel powered.

The track recording systems vehicle has banks of screens allowing operators to view a range of system outputs, including track faults, train location, and radio signal strength.

The NMT is being used to inform the design of the next generation of high-speed trains to be introduced in the UK. In particular research is underway on regenerative braking – this recovers energy which would otherwise be lost when a train brakes. So far this type of ground breaking technology has only been attempted by the Japanese in lower speed commuter trains.

A trial is being conducted using the New Measurement Train and involving Network Rail, Hitachi and Porterbrook. Following extensive commissioning and testing since the train was completed in April of this year it is now to commence work in service. Data will be collected and analysed to validate the computer predicted energy savings of at least 20 percent in fuel, to research optimum battery capacity, and study interface, technology and safety factors. It is anticipated that this work will be completed within a year and the headline results released to the industry.

It is estimated that a 100kWh battery on a train running 220,000 miles per year will deliver a saving 68,662 tonnes of CO_2.

Figure D

It's just gone 0600 hours and NMT (with 43014) waits to form the 1C00 0619 departure from Paddington to Taunton. This wasn't my shift so I must have popped out early from my hotel for the shot. I'd kept my tripod in the train for several weeks hoping I'd get the chance, but usually there wasn't enough time or we were put into another platform where a clear shot wasn't possible. 17 March 2007.

Inside the NMT Production Vehicle (977994) at night. The lead OTT would sit on the left, communicating with the driver using the handheld radio and logging any issues (such as faults and lost recording mileage) on the daily spreadsheet on the lower screen. The track recorder would sit in the middle of the table to operate the video cameras, observe the Tracksys system and RTPS, resyncing when required and passing details of track faults to the lead. The performance of the laser system cameras could be monitored on the far right screens. 12 March 2011.

No. 43014 leads the NMT around the curve and under the familiar road bridge at Teignmouth, returning to Paddington from Plymouth with Gary Payne in charge. This was another popular trip for visitors to the train to select, assuming they could get to Paddington for the early start. 18 June 2010.

5
Hitachi's *Hayabusa*

The NMT was used as a suitable test bed for a hybrid traction system developed by Hitachi, in collaboration with Brush Traction and Porterbrook. With the forthcoming IET in mind, this used a large set of batteries that would get a train under way from station stops in a more efficient and environmentally friendly manner than with sole use of a loco's diesel engine, in this case the Paxman Valenta in an HST power car. Its engine management system would start the diesel at around 20mph, which would then gradually assume full traction in place of the batteries. The a.c. traction motors were configured to provide regenerative charging during

Quorn station on the Great Central Railway is the setting for this view from the initial testing of the Brush/Hitachi hybrid power system on an HST. 43089 *Hayabusa* is coupled to 977996, in which the batteries are situated. Acting as support vehicle, Track Lab 977974 is behind with normally configured power car 43160 at the rear. 1 June 2007.

A case of old technologies meeting new. Parked briefly in front of the GCR's Loughborough workshop, HST power car No. 43089 enjoys the sunshine. Once returned to normal front-line service for East Midlands Trains, it would later be passing through Loughborough frequently, of course, but on the Midland Railway's route. 23 May 2007.

Right: Close-up of the nameplate and cast falcon on the side of 43089. The power car inevitably became known as 'high abuser' amongst the technicians, though it never really caused us many problems to be fair!

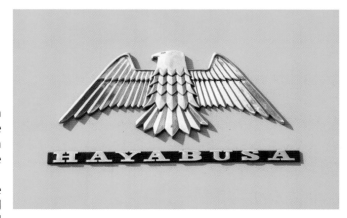

braking. The size and quantity of the batteries was such that they had to be accommodated in a separate vehicle to the Class 43 power car (in this case Mark 3 coach No. 977996) but this also meant that it could readily be returned to the general HST fleet afterwards.

Hayabusa is Japanese for peregrine falcon and the nameplate on the side of power car No. 43089 harked back to that on the Class 53 locomotive D0280, produced by Brush in 1961.

Initial testing with support vehicle 977974 (still known as Track Lab) and standard power car 43160 took place at the Great Central Railway in May 2007 before *Hayabusa* and its battery coach were inserted into the NMT formation that August for main line testing up to full line speed. Use of the hybrid power car in the NMT continued on and off until the following September, when it was returned to Brush prior to joining the East Midlands Trains fleet. 43089 was later fitted with a Paxman VP185 power unit in common with the rest of the EMT power cars.

Overleaf: Having arrived from Ayr (with the train handed over to the next team), this was one occasion when I had time to walk down from Crewe station and take up a position opposite the LNWR shed to capture the train leaving for Euston. With six vehicles in the rake and 43089 *Hayabusa* leading, the NMT looks impressive indeed as it wends its way over Crewe South Junction and on to the up fast line, Steve Suddaby at the controls. The blue lining on the side of the train was no longer being applied by this time and gradually disappeared from the rest of the vehicles as they received heavy maintenance. 7 May 2008.

I may have had a hotel to go to in Leeds on this particular Monday evening, as I'd normally have been on my way home after the shift change. We'd brought the train off Heaton that morning, then recorded across to Newcastle for a southbound run over the S&C. The practice was for the NMT to record north over the S&C on the following Saturday. The second shift are now onboard waiting to take the train onwards to York and I've waited around for them to pass back westward on their way to Manchester. 11 February 2008.

TRC Steps in for NMT

By June 2006, the pairing of Mark 3 Production and Development Vehicles within NMT was achieved, allowing TRC to be returned to use in its own loco-hauled formation. However, there were many teething troubles with the new track recording software on PV so TRC would often substitute for NMT.

'HSTRC' (High Speed Track Recording Coach, as it was originally known) had been introduced into service by BR's chief civil engineer in 1978. It was the last Mark 2 vehicle to emerge from Derby's Litchurch Lane Works but the first TRV in Britain to employ an inertial measurement-based track recording system that was capable of recording dynamically at full line speed. It initiated the retirement of regional track recording cars that employed an older versine-based system plus a fleet of Matisa 'Neptune' track recording trolleys dating from the late 1950s that could only work at low speed on main lines (there is a very interesting British Pathe video about these online); the introduction of TRU, with equipment similar to TRC's, for lesser routes ten years later completed the job. Equipment

No. 31285 sets out from Crewe for Glasgow with TRC, substituting for the NMT. Need I add that the smoke at the rear wasn't emanating from the Virgin 'Thunderbird' Class 57s (but from 31233)? 12 July 2006.

The down refuge siding at Crewe South Junction was a favourite place to put test trains for shift changes, if they couldn't be held at the station. I quite enjoyed the walk down past the old diesel depot and through the bushes to get to the train. The track underneath 37608 looks modern enough but go beyond the rear loco (37609) towards the buffer stop and you'd come across some very old rail chairs. These two 37s are about to get nicely warmed up as they'd take us non-stop to Euston and back on the fast lines only 157½ miles away, according to the milepost. 7 March 2007.

on TRC and TRU was updated towards the end of the 1990s by the introduction of the Serco-Lewis Digital Track Geometry System, named after the engineer Ray Lewis and the company then responsible for operating the IM fleet. Although TRC was initially a self-contained unit, only needing to be coupled up to normal service trains or included in multiple-unit formations, by this period it no longer had generators or onboard staff accommodation and therefore usually ran in company with support vehicle DB977337.

At first, top-and-tail EWS Class 67s powered the TRC rake but at £3,000 per loco per shift, that didn't last very long. First recourse was to our own Class 31s but their range (not to mention their performance) proved a limiting factor, therefore on we progressed to DRS Class 37/6s. These did their best to maintain the NMT timings, but again it was asking a lot of 40-year-old locomotives limited to 90mph to try and stick to something intended for a train that cruised at 100 plus. We still saw 67s on occasion, though I got the impression that only happened if the departmental budget permitted!

On Monday, 11 September 2006, 37607 and 608 were working TRC from Derby to Edinburgh. All was well until Doncaster, when 607 refused to produce power past

the first field divert (or so the driver explained to me!). He decided to press on with only 608 pushing until that too began to overheat while running at speed. This led to the fire alarm going off inside the train, which meant we had to radio the cab to stop the train. A check in Chevington loop that all was well on the loco allowed us to continue on to Grantshouse loop, where we were due to stop anyway. 608's engine was shut down to help it cool for the duration. Once under way again, the fire alarm still sounded repeatedly, until the driver just asked us if we minded if he pressed on to Edinburgh and sanctuary (?) at Craigentinny. I think we must have stuffed toilet paper into the alarm in TRC to make the noise more bearable! Unfortunately nobody had told the depot we were coming and for some reason they were refusing to allow access for the DRS fitter, who'd been sent out to us, to attend to the loco. So back we went into Waverley, where a new part was fitted to 607, bringing that loco back to life and thus relieving the burden on 608. The recording leg onwards to Glasgow Queen Street had to be caped as we were two hours down; fun and games indeed.

There were two more working shifts for me to do with our 'cooking' 37s in what turned out to be a more eventful week than usual. On my way from Newcastle to

Manchester on the Tuesday, I joined the NMT at Carlisle as an observer during pantograph testing on the Development Vehicle. Over two days, the train ran to test sites near Low Gill and Milnthorpe to run at 20mph on some tight curvature, thereby creating the conditions where the pan was most likely to slip off the contact wire. They didn't appear to experience any problems with that on my visit, though I did notice that one of the power cars was out of action – no change there then!

On the Wednesday morning, I was back on TRC out of Longsight doing the track recording run to Glasgow that the NMT would normally have done and we passed them still doing their pan tests south of Carlisle, amidst a chorus of horns. The local track engineer had been concerned about the state of the slab track in Queen Street Tunnel and needed to see regular geometry data for it so, because we'd missed that piece of recording on the Monday, we were required to make a diversion across the City Union line to get to that, instead of the normal run into Glasgow Central. The route was Larkfield Jn–Shields Jn–High Street Jn–Bellgrove Jn–Sighthill East Jn–Cowlairs South Jn–Queen St and return. This was traversing a part of Glasgow

Above: Serco driver Colin Campbell is on the phone to Control from the cab of a very clean 37610 at Rugby. The loco was partnering 37609 with TIC and operating as a substitute for the NMT. 14 July 2005.

Below: This is platform 18 at Euston, right over on the west side of the terminus and a stone's throw from the Thistle Hotel (where we sometimes overnighted before or after a shift). No. 67006 *Royal Sovereign* (with 67025 at the rear) has brought TRC from Derby and I'm one of the relieving team who will work it to Manchester and Crewe that evening. Phil McDermott has just alighted and seems to be giving me an ironic wave! HS2 work would alter this side of the station. 6 October 2006.

TRC, running in place of NMT, sits in Manchester Piccadilly just after midnight with 37606 and 37612 in charge. This was 1Z95 from Derby RTC to Longsight, which ran via Lichfield Trent Valley, Euston and Crewe to record the WCML slow lines. 6 February 2007.

I'd not seen before (not the most picturesque, it must be said), though our two locos made a lovely noise climbing back up the 1 in 42 out of Queen Street. I overnighted at Crewe and was able to make a quick visit home on Thursday before going on to London, ready for Friday morning's Paddington to Plymouth run, which passed off without a hitch.

Further pairings of locos on the TRC I experienced included 31106/233, 31106/602, 31128/47703, 37610/611, 67006/029. Even TRC wasn't always available to stand in for the NMT and back in November 2004 Dave Smith, Mike New and I spent an entire night shift running between Rugby and Euston on TIC with Class 67s, as the requirement for geometry data on the WCML had become so pressing. TIC was already doing a week of daytime working out of Hither Green but was deemed available for this emergency. My notes read as follows:

'We should have started from Hither Green at 19.00 but left an hour late, due to awaiting the EWS crew (who have to drive the TIC formation when using 67s). The task was to record all four tracks between Euston and Rugby and we lost further time throughout the night (for various

reasons, probably possessions). We also ran out of CDs on which to record all the data. Hopes of finishing and detraining at Wembley Yard at 04.30 were dashed when a taxi couldn't be provided for us so we had to stay onboard all the way back to Hither Green again. Using early morning commuter trains to Blackheath (where our hotel was) took a while, though we arrived just in time for breakfast. I managed three hours sleep and then checked my phone for messages: It seemed I needed to go down to Three Bridges to meet the TIC again in order to get the data from the previous night, which had since been recorded on to some freshly supplied CDs, brought by the team on that day's shift. That done, I headed home via Kings Cross, where I handed the CDs to Dave, as he was going back via the office. The data needed to be verified that evening; otherwise the track maintainer would have been in line for a substantial penalty payment!'

At Christmas 2006, the new geometry system on NMT (Tracksys) was signed off for productive use but one week into the New Year we were back to using TRC. It wasn't until the autumn of 2007 that the odd pairings of locos plus TRC (in place of NMT) became a real rarity once again.

Opposite top: Some further views of TRC workings; it must go down as one of the most successful of test vehicles! No. 73138 (with 73107 at rear) pauses with a rake of coaches that includes TRC at Kilburn High Road working 1Q76, the 2143 Selhurst–Selhurst, via Watford Junction. I can't remember the reason for stopping here but suspect it was due to a possession up ahead. Note the headlight and camera located in the loco's headcode box, intended for use with the third rail Electrification Monitoring Vehicle (EMV). 12 February 2011.

Opposite bottom: 73107 with TRC, seen from the gates to the MoD facility at Ludgershall. Track recording on freight-only branches could be an imprecise affair inasmuch as the recording of data didn't always exactly finish at the point where responsibility for track maintenance passed from Network Rail to the terminal owner. 10 January 2012.

Above: The view across Poole Harbour from TRC, a nice payback for an early start. 11 January 2012.

Overleaf: Not long after sunrise on 11 January 2012, 73138 and 201 double head TRC towards Poole while operating as 1Q43 06.30 Eastleigh–Eastleigh (via Weymouth). The train had just completed its first recording run of the day on the Hamworthy Quay branch; not quite an hour before, we'd waited on the main line for permission to go on to the branch and watched that incredibly colourful dawn over Poole Harbour.

People and Trains

Above: Inside the conference coach of NMT at Barrow Hill sidings during a calibration run between there and Derby in 2003: While the rostered team worked in the Track Recording Coach, Arthur Richards (on the right) was giving a group of spare OTTs the benefit of some of his vast experience so that they might start their new role on the train with a better feel for interpreting track geometry charts. One that has just been recorded is displayed on the screen behind. Clockwise from the left we have Ashleigh Frost, Phil McDermott, Carl Andrews, Andy Morris, Richard Head, Mike New, Dave Smith and Arthur. Dave Green is the driver on the ballast, changing ends.

Opposite top: NMT has just completed its return run from St Pancras to Bedford and will shortly go back to Derby on the fasts with Andy Wylde driving 43062. MML traffic was using the eastern side of the remodelled station as an interim arrangement before switching permanently to the west side. The gas holder in the background would also be getting moved to a new home a few hundred yards north from here. 27 April 2006.

Opposite bottom: AEA Technology engineers prepare to mount the control module for the Cybernetix track monitoring system underneath the NMT Development Vehicle 977993 at the RTC. The idea was that an array of cameras would be kept 'in sync' with the track, compensating for the motion of the vehicle. Object recognition software would then be employed to assess the images recorded and flag up anomalies (e.g. broken or displaced track components) for the on-train staff to make a judgement on. A different (and less complex) system was later trialled and put into everyday use on the PLPR fleet of vehicles, as well as NMT itself.

Opposite top: On 6 January 2009, there was time for a photo during a pathing stop of the TRC at Barmouth. George Jones and Alan Guest are the two drivers while my fellow OTT on the right is Mike New. George had been in the Royal Navy and Alan had been on patrol cars with West Midlands Police – I imagine driving a Class 37 was rather different to driving a Rover 3500! I returned that August onboard RSC3, which tested GSMR in preparation for the introduction of ERTMS on the Cambrian ... and only those yellow class 97/3s would be allowed.

Opposite bottom: Well I've got to include this shot, haven't I? *Pandora* meets NMT in platform 1 at Crewe – let the smoking contest begin! I'm working on the NMT and we've just come south from Stockport, heading back to Derby via Stoke. I can only think that we're not due to leave just yet and the box have decided to let the bubble car in on top of us. The opportunity for some banter between train crews is clearly not being wasted. 17 February 2006.

Above: At a time when the NMT ran up the WCML to Glasgow every week, Preston was the location for a mid-afternoon shift change. The early shift took the train off Longsight around 0530 and handed over to the late shift here at 1500, the train ending up back at the RTC between 0100 and 0200 the following morning. It wasn't unusual for the train to detect a reportable fault around Preston North Junction, in which case there would have to be a hurried exchange of information from one crew to the other as an impatient driver up front waited under a green signal. Mike New, Dave Smith and Carl Andrews are seen on the platform. Comedian Frank Carson was sat near to us once as the train rolled in; 'NEW Measurement Train? What's new about it?' I heard him say. Oh no, not you too, Frank! 27 July 2005.

Above: I'm not sure who the two nearest drivers are (or which pair is taking over from which!) but Chris Dissanayake and Wally Wright are the two facing the camera late one evening at Kings Cross. I will have joined the train mid-afternoon at Doncaster and come south with it before running out to Grantham and back on the 'slows'. Now I'm heading to my hotel and maybe some sleep.

Right: Drivers Paul Clark and Brian George (in cab) at Glasgow Central; Paul was learning NMT on the Derby–Crewe–Glasgow–Carstairs–Craigentinny turn, though they would only have driven part of that. 1 March 2011.

Opposite: Tony Birks (shunter), Steve Simpkin (fitter) and Brian Gott (driver) watch closely as NMT is re-formed in the RTC yard at Derby. Sidings and space in general were at a premium here so whenever the NMT was around for technical work or coaches needed rearranging the yard staff often had their work cut out. 30 July 2011.

Above: The advantage of being able to clean the cameras in an inspection pit was that you could get close enough to see what you were doing, instead of being at arm's length when lying alongside the train in a siding. From this view it can be seen how much of the wheel tyre is in normal contact with the rail head – perhaps not as much as some might expect! 10 November 2008.

Left: Driver Darren Harris phones the box on the then single-line section between Ascott-under-Wychwood and Wolvercot Junction. Serco required NMT drivers to wear collar and tie. 22 April 2009.

Opposite top: John Bradley leans across to give the camera box a wipe at Kilmarnock. Did we risk assess that beforehand? I can't remember ... 28 October 2009.

Opposite bottom: Checking the optical fibre connections between the NMT coaches and power car 43013 at Hereford (fuelling sidings) – Daves Tully and Smith are on to it and (hopefully) a better-quality video feed will be the result! All the doors on the NMT carried the 'Not for public use' message but it was surprising how often passengers tried to get on at some stations. 16 September 2009.

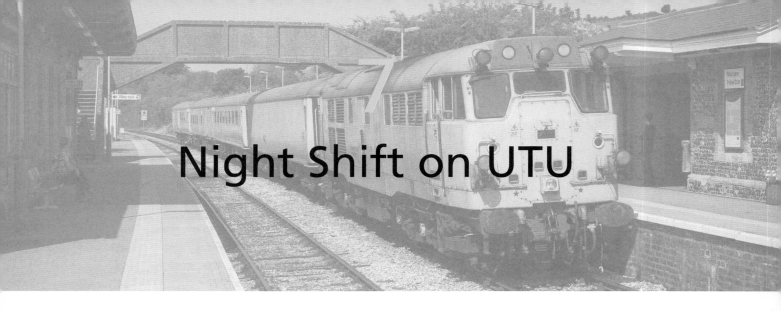

Night Shift on UTU

I n July 2007, our roster was changed and in a big way. The operating schedule of the NMT had already altered in the new May timetable, with reduced frequency of recording of the main routes and the addition of some new ones that had previously been covered by TRU or TIC. However, the new roster involved the pooling of staff from all trains and that affected me immediately – for eight weeks, I was assigned to UTU4! Although there had been practically no consultation with any of us beforehand, the aim was clearly to get everyone trained on all the

trains – fine in principle, but in practice I think most on-train staff would have had their own views on why perhaps this wasn't such a good idea.

Work on the ultrasonic test trains was typically one week on and one week off. That looked OK on paper but if, like me, you don't always take kindly to being up all night, then you find you need that alternate week off just to normalise the body clock. I had done all-night shifts before, of course but only in isolation. My first week on UTU4 was five nights' work in a row. So on the Monday

The first ultrasonic test coach to bear the title UTU2 was originally one of the last Mark 1 coaches built for BR in 1974. Initially carrying the number 62482 (from its days as part of a 4REP EMU), it was renumbered 999605 and later became UTUS (spare) when ex-4CIG coach 62287 assumed the title UTU2 (having been configured internally to an improved standard in line with the rest of the UTU fleet). The measuring bogie is on the right, where two fluorescent lights are mounted on the solebar to assist preparation of the vehicle prior to nightly operations. It is shown at the RTC on 6 April 2006.

Late on Friday, 19 December 2008, 31233 ticks over prior to departure from St Philips Marsh depot. Note the small camera window fitted into the loco's sealed up gangway door aperture. UTU3 (999602) has been prepared for duty and will be operated back to Derby over the Lickey route.

afternoon I made my way to the very quiet and weed-strewn EWS depot at Old Oak Common, its heyday of maintaining express train motive power now long passed. With plenty of time to spare, I was able to have a leisurely depot induction from one of the skeleton staff there, a chat with someone else who had been at Barrow Hill shed the previous week for a Class 20 gala and then took a wander among all the stored Class 56s that were parked around the old turntable. UTU4 (coach No. 999606) was nearby formed up with its two DRS Class 37s at either end.

Presently, my NR buddy for the night, Mel Martin, appeared along with the two Sperry technicians who would accompany me for the rest of the week. Our task for that night was to record the fasts between Paddington and Reading (less than 70 miles in total), before making a transit move across north London to Ilford depot. Mel showed me that the NR train manager's job wasn't the most onerous one onboard but having to physically poke my head out of the window to see the mileposts coming wasn't much to my liking – the track recording fleet was better adapted for that purpose. And in winter time, I imagined this would be a very cold job to perform, even at the train's modest operating speed of 30mph! The preparation of a UTU vehicle took the longest of any monitoring train in my opinion, as the two Sperry employees gave more than just a cursory check of their

equipment. They made a close inspection and detailed check of every working part of the bogie-mounted gear to minimise the chance of failure during the shift, usually getting thoroughly dirty in the process. Arranging for the siding's protection and liaising with the driver – my principal tasks – seemed the cushier role! It proved an uneventful shift, punctuated by the expected yawns and the odd snack as we made our way haltingly to a siding at the rear of Ilford depot. Finally checking in to a hotel at first light was clearly going to become a habit I'd have to get used to.

Mel left me on my own for the rest of the week and I managed OK, apart from one run where I confused Hornsey station for Alexandra Palace (when starting to monitor the Hertford loop) and the only solution was to radio the driver to stop the train. It was a touch embarrassing at the time but the driver was fine with it and afterwards I was quite pleased with myself for not panicking. I'd done the right thing. Possibly we'd slightly delayed a late evening commuter train behind us while I recreated a computer data file; however, the alternative would have been a stream of data tagged with the wrong positions and a real headache for the data processors. Earlier that same night, a late start from Ilford had been avoided by me arranging for a fire-damaged Class 321 unit to be moved from its position where it had been

The control desk inside UTU3 (999602), looking from the Sperry technicians' side. The NR OTT would sit opposite. The joystick box is in front of various screens providing information on how the ultrasonic gear was functioning and what data was being produced. December 2008.

blocking us into our siding. That involved a number of phone calls, an amount of walking back and forth across the yard and cajoling the Sperry guys into stopping their prep work while the unit was shunted. I guess I was settling into my new role quite well.

It was certainly taking me out of my comfort zone of the NMT. Being the sole NR employee on a UTU, sometimes you found yourself making your way alone to a train parked in an unfamiliar place. For example, the Euston down sidings carriage neck was a favourite place to stable prior to a late shift but I'd never been there before and it's a long walk off the end of platform 19 in the dark. Unnervingly, the walking route lights came to an end with no sign of any train and only the faintest glow from the nearby streetlights. I'd been assured it was there so kept walking until finally a pair of red lights began to glimmer through the trackside buddleia – my train, I presumed. A little while later, I recounted all this to a driver and he told me he'd walked the same way one evening and heard a shout from above. He looked up and saw somebody pointing a gun at him!

A night stabled in Peterborough and another in Cambridge before finishing at Derby early on the Saturday morning

saw us to the end of that week. The highlight for me was being invited to ride in the cab of 37059 by the driver on the way back from Peterborough. I won't forget the throbbing and vibration from that engine, particularly as we forged through the darkness and plunged into Stamford Tunnel with the power controller opened wide. All the signal boxes that we passed en route were manned, so it kind of felt like a train journey of old. It's only when you get to ride in the cab of a train at night that you start to understand the job that train drivers do and why knowledge of the route is so important. Having to drive at line speed when you can see little of what's ahead of you (except perhaps when approaching a colour light signal) has to require some degree of accustomisation and sheer nerve. I would guess the feeling is the same in conditions of thick fog because if there should happen to be something immovable on the line in front of you, you're going to hit it. That's something that the general public probably don't appreciate.

My second week took me up to Scotland for four nights doing a section of the WCML, the GSW route to Kilmarnock and the Stranraer line. This necessitated me having two hotel rooms booked simultaneously in two different towns

– Carlisle and Ayr. The first night we recorded from Weaver Jn to Tebay loop, where we had to stop for the Sperry lads to change a burst Roller Searcher Unit (RSU, that's the little inflatable rubber tyre enclosing the ultrasonic probes); then over Shap for us to get off the train at Carlisle, while it carried on as ECS to Ayr. That meant we had to travel to Ayr the following evening, ready for a midnight departure to Stranraer, for which we had the line under our possession south of Kilkerran. The driver Rob McKay, a Scotsman who I had only met once before, wanted me to help him do a brake test on the train. This presented a problem; although I had done this in training five years back, I couldn't remember the procedure precisely and conditions weren't favourable. I had a bit of a job understanding Rob's thick Glaswegian accent when stood in front of him, let alone on the end of a fuzzy two-way radio whilst being next to an idling Class 37! It was dark and I had a heavy torch with a failing battery in the other hand so that didn't help my straining to catch Rob's instructions. All the same, he was very patient with me and we managed the test; after a phone call to Mel the next day to discuss it, I was much happier doing it the following night; seeing the brake blocks going on and off the wheels of the loco was the reassurance you looked for, above all. Our timings for

Stranraer showed us recording the main line on the way down and the loops on the way back. Simple enough you might think, it was just a problem knowing for sure which track was the loop at some of these passing places (the Quail maps weren't always the gospel truth) and it seemed the signallers hadn't necessarily left the points set for the main tracks anyway.

As on the track recording trains, the information collected on the UTU had to be labelled with accurate positional data so the job of the NR person was to resync the computer against the mileposts intermittently, not to mention keeping the rest of the crew supplied with hot tea or coffee. In contrast, one of the Sperry technicians' constant tasks was to keep the RSUs positioned centrally on the rail via a pair of joysticks on their control desk; otherwise, the ultrasonic waves couldn't penetrate to the foot of the rail and achieve the optimum assessment of it. I was told that for most of the time, the task was to ensure that existing flaws in the rails were not getting worse rather than actually detecting new ones, hence the need for regular monitoring (maybe it's not widely understood that despite improvements over the years, there are still impurities in new steel rails that can instigate flaws). It was also important to be ready to lift the RSUs on the

Two main pieces of equipment are of interest here on the underside of UTU4 (999606) at Exeter Riverside: On the left (with the yellow warning sticker) is Ground-Penetrating Radar and in the middle are the KLD system cameras, inspecting the profile of the rails using the lighting array around them. GPR is used to check the state of the formation below the track, whilst KLD will flag up excessively worn rails. The outward facing lamp at the top assists the crew in spotting mileposts. 25 August 2009.

The monitoring bogie on UTU1 (62384). With the vehicle running left to right, the left-hand RSU is deployed with water sprayed ahead of it – a dampness on the side of the rail can be seen from this operation at the moment the train stopped. The RSU next to it is the spare and the two to the right would be used when the train reversed. The heavy construction of these former EMU bogies provides a very solid platform for mounting all the necessary monitoring equipment, including Ground-Penetrating Radar. 25 March 2015.

approach to complex S&C layouts, as experience had shown these were the areas where lipping and uneven wear of the rail heads produced sharp edges that could easily burst the RSU tyre. A back-up RSU was always ready to lower should that happen but the UTUs tended to concentrate on plain line work, leaving the S&C areas to be assessed manually with the equipment referred to as 'walking sticks'. The other technician would also be continually checking a screen that showed the output from the probes, ready to call out anything serious that might need us to close the line to traffic.

To help keep them alert, one of the team had rigged up a small hi-fi system to play his favourite music; so there we were, trundling through the pitch dark and very empty Galloway countryside at one in the morning to the sound of Abba singing 'SOS' … I have to admit I found myself singing along with the rest.

All went smoothly until just short of Barrhill, when the brakes came on sharply and Rob's voice came over the radio, effing and blinding. 'Uh oh, he's not sounding too happy,' said John Reeves (one of the Sperry pair), which apart from stating the obvious also indicated that perhaps I wasn't the only one who didn't quite understand all the detail of Rob's messages. No matter, I looked out of the

window and could see a clutch of people in hi-viz orange jackets around the signal post ahead of us. It transpired that we weren't alone in our supposedly exclusive possession, hence Rob's annoyance as nobody had told him to expect this. I suppose it counted as a near miss but I wasn't going to be the one to make a fuss over it. Anyway, having let them know in no uncertain terms that they shouldn't have been there, Rob told them he'd forget the incident provided they weren't there when we came back from Stranraer. And that was the end of it.

The following night took us back to Carlisle again. A beautiful sunrise to the east as we passed through Annan was nice, though scant compensation for our latest finish yet; 0630 hours! Leaving the station, I walked through the deserted shopping centre of Carlisle and up to the Crown & Mitre Hotel on English Street … just in time for breakfast. I imagined this wouldn't be the last time I'd be eating bacon and eggs just before bed.

Helpfully for me though, before coming home from Ayr on the Saturday, I had had an additional (Friday) night booked for me at the Fairfield House Hotel to begin returning to a normal pattern of sleep, plus an opportunity to enjoy a pint of Guinness before my evening meal without the concern of having to go on shift! Talking

One or two detail differences can be noted between these otherwise similar vehicles: DBS (Driving Brake Staff) coaches 9701 and 9714 are in the yard at Exeter Riverside, working with RSC1 (977868) and UTU4 (999606), together with locos 31465 and 31602. 25 August 2009.

subsequently to the staff who normally worked the UTUs, I discovered I wasn't alone in taking several days to readjust my body clock to normal sleep patterns. I'd been unhappy to do those night shifts at first, but it felt good to look back on them with a sense of achievement. And I knew that I could do that work again if it came to it ... which, it inevitably did after a while.

The last week of shifts I did on a UTU stuck in my memory as it was in the middle of winter. With temperatures well below zero, our running was interrupted by the RSU water sprays freezing up. I was just relieved that it wasn't down to me to don the dirty orange overalls and go underneath the train to thaw them out. It was one of my duties, however to plan ahead and think about when we might need to replenish the water tanks; although it was only a small spray of water (required to act as 'couplant' between the ultrasonic probes and the rail head), it was surprising how quickly a thousand litres of water was spent. The tank on 999602 (UTU3) was a big one, so you knew you could go for several

nights without topping up but the other vehicles (just 999605 and 999606 at that time) had less capacity – sometimes you'd be running out on the second night with them. No. 999602 was actually the original UTU vehicle introduced in 1992 that ran between two Met-Cam driving cars, carrying the set number 901001. It succeeded the ultrasonic test train two-car DMU, dating from 1970 when ultrasonic testing was first undertaken by a train.

If we weren't able to fill up at any stabling point, it was a big help to have a driver who knew where the watering points for passenger stock were in the larger stations and then try to get us routed into the right platform. I think it was in Euston station one night where we struggled to align the filler on the coach with the watering point; I was stood on the platform issuing instructions to the driver over the radio and trying to judge the correct braking point for him. Not easy, up and down the platform we went: 'Five yards, two yards ... STOP! No, that's too far. Back again ...'

Dave Talbot brings 31285 with a combined train of two UTU sets back from calibration at Old Dalby, 31602 bringing up the rear. Interesting track alignment here! 13 June 2011.

Above: Just after midnight in Milton Keynes' bay platform 2A, 31105 prepares to depart southwards along the up slow with a working of UTU2 (999605) as 3Q68 2150 Euston Down Carriage Shed Neck–Old Oak Common HST Depot. Accompanying UTU2 are generator 6263 and DBS 9702. The driver is Tony Falloon. 30 July 2013.

Opposite top: UTU1 (62384) arrives at Maiden Newton behind 31233 (observed by my wife on the left!). The pathing of trains over this route was such that a UTU train, running at monitoring speed, could comfortably be fitted in during the day. This working was 3Z14 10.05 Westbury–Didcot (via Weymouth). By this date, most monitoring trains had a 'Q' in the headcode (to help alert signalling staff that they had to adhere to planned routes as much as possible). However, for some obscure reason certain signalling equipment in the Western zone didn't recognise 'Q' and so 'Z' would still get used on some affected test trains. DB977986 (behind the loco) was not only windowless but completely bereft of fittings inside. 27 August 2013.

Opposite bottom: A hired-in 31106 in BR blue livery trundles into the seaside terminus at Skegness with driver Nigel Walls at the controls, returning a taste of how trains often used to look here. The train is UTU1 (62384), formed up with generator van 6264 and DBS 9702, running as 3Q01 0900 from Derby RTC and return. Rob Cook was the lead OTT that day and I took the opportunity to chat to him and inspect the interior of the recently fitted out UTU1. Drivers and OTTs alike hoped that the timings might allow a trip to the chippie whenever Skegness featured in the roster – it didn't always happen. 1 April 2013.

8

Driver Dave Green

To mark his long career on the railway, a Class 31 on hire to Network Rail for test train operation was named *Driver Dave Green* during a surprise ceremony at the Railway Technical Centre in Derby on 3 November 2007. Fleet Engineer Bill Hunt introduced proceedings by stating that the occasion also marked fifty years in service of the Class 31. Driver Jason Rogers then said a few words on behalf of his colleagues before Dave received from his son a mounted replica of the nameplate (and 19B shedplate) that he'd just unveiled on 31602. No. 19B was the shedcode for Sheffield Millhouses depot where Dave first started work.

Stood in front of 31602, Jason Rogers says a few words to Dave Green while his son waits to present the mounted replica nameplate. As you can see, it looks as if Dave has turned up for work without suspecting that the day would be much different to any other! Driver Manager Paul Verghese is on the left of shot, fleet engineer Bill Hunt is to the right. 3 November 2007.

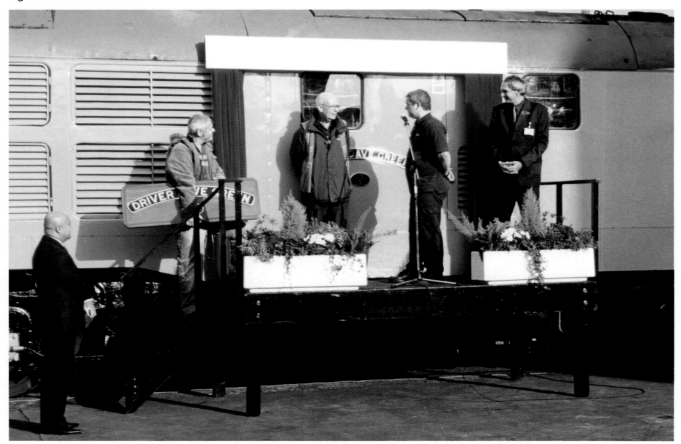

After the nameplate had been unveiled on 31602, a group photo was staged. Most of the test train drivers were there, together with support staff from the office, the yard and the EDU; all played their part in making rail travel safe in this country!

And a year after the naming of the loco, here is the man himself on the platform at his home town of Sheffield, just as he'd completed his last driving turn on the network. 8 November 2008.

As I was PTS qualified, I was able to walk from the station through the RTC yard on my way to and from the office (in Trent House). With luck, something interesting might be parked in a position for a decent photo: Here we have 31602 *Driver Dave Green* showing some of the equipment it had received for working the SGT; although a couple of infrared lights are mounted on its cab roof, the camera in the nose window seems to have been removed. Note also the lack of a Network Rail logo on this loco, as it was never owned by the company. As I write these words (in 2018), the loco is being scrapped at Wolsingham. 7 October 2010.

Coupled up to the inspection saloon *Amanda*, 31602 was later taken on a mini-tour to Leicester and back with 31459 in support. I daresay that only tea and coffee was on offer in the saloon and maybe some cake!

Dave retired from the railway almost exactly one year later.

Staff in the group photo are as follows: Rosanna Lysaczenko (office manager), Clive Barlow, (controller), Steve Hayden (controller), Jason Rogers, Mick Stewart (engineer), Billy Hilton, (shunter), Pete Erwin (engineer), Andy Beddoe, Chris Hewitt, Jason Dicks, Richard O'Connor, Terry Coyne, Steve Sheehan, Steve Suddaby, Mick Paszke, Phil Devonport, Ken Keegan (shunter), Sean Dunne, Ben Deeley, Linda Green (Dave's wife), Dave Talbot, Colin Hayward, Paul Clark, Steve Smithies (operations manager), Franz Latchford (maintenance manager), Alan Guest, Chris Jennings, Jo Coultas, Richard Sargent, Ian Thurman, Dave Green, Richard Waterhouse, Wally Wright, Andy Parker, Gary Payne, Ian Tennant, Darren Harris, Tony Angel, Paul Verghese (driver manager), John Maddock, Brian Allison, Rob McKay, Bill Hunt (engineer), Ian Bayliss (controller), Jonathan Thame, Mick Gray, Steve Hazelwood, Brian Gott and Martin Tanner.

Dave was one of a team of around forty drivers. They signed some or all of the following traction: TRU, NMT, Class 31, 37, 67, 73, 97/3 plus the DBS and DVT. Any other traction tended to require external drivers to be drafted in – that could make life interesting for the OTTs because the external drivers

didn't always appreciate our needs. Over time, enough test train drivers were employed with route knowledge to cover the whole country so that conductors from other operators were then only brought in at times of staff shortage.

Test train drivers were quite a cross-section of characters, mostly experienced but ranging from men in their twenties to those (like Dave) approaching retirement. There were some who just regarded it as another driving job but I would say that most did it because they valued the opportunity to do a variety of work, whether that meant different motive power or being able to drive along different routes. Whilst some were happy to stick to a limited amount of route knowledge, others seemed to be looking to expand theirs – it was said that one individual was able to 'sign' the whole of Scotland! The majority seemed keen to go the extra mile when needed to, something that often came to the fore when you are talking about trains that tend to run irregularly.

I always felt that it was important to keep on good terms with them and took time to ensure they had mugs of tea or coffee when required, especially if there wasn't the chance for them to leave the cab to make their own. Whilst some liked to chat with the OTTs throughout the journey, sometimes asking over the radio whether a poor piece of track had registered on the computer, others would happily drive non-stop for hours without a word, even when they were alone up front.

A Substitute for TRU

I could see this one coming on the all-singing, all-dancing roster: three late shifts in South Wales to record all of the valleys and the branch lines. And I mean ALL of them. Normally this would have been another job for the TRU but as the dates drew nearer, the unit was showing no signs of moving from the depths of the EDU workshop and the week previously the venerable TIC (999508) had been sent down to Cornwall between two Class 37s to tidy up the other branches we'd not covered in September.

Not only was TRU being prepared for a video survey run but it still had to do its annual calibration runs and they couldn't wait for its return to service. Sure enough, the decision was taken to leave TIC at Bristol over the weekend for our stint, so down I went to Temple Meads on the Monday (7 April 2008).

The 'coach' was sat sandwiched by 37059/218 in a siding next to platform 15 that used to be the loco access line to Bath Road diesel depot, the site of which was now

The Severn Tunnel and South Wales awaits TIC on the afternoon of 8 April 2008 at Bristol Temple Meads, with 37218 and 059 doing the honours; power to weight ratio was quite high, I would say. The abandoned Post Office block and disused mail conveyor bridge provide a backdrop to the train here; once a prime route on to Bath Road depot, this siding was often used by test trains.

The track recorder's position on the TIC (999508) was something of a cobbled together arrangement. With the swivel chair in place, it wasn't possible to easily access the rest of the computer rack behind it. But provided everything worked correctly, that didn't normally matter. The VDU screen angled above didn't make for the most ergonomic arrangement but with that wall heater, this was comfortably the warmest place to be on cold winter nights. Your colleague kept warm through constant movement and supplying you with hot drinks from the galley.

I spent six days on one particular Scottish tour, which should have used the TRU all week. However, the DMU wasn't available to start with so they sent TIC up on a Sunday with top and tail 37s. Luckily for me, I didn't have to travel up on it from Derby – instead I got to Edinburgh by GNER on the Monday. Early Tuesday morning, we worked as 2Q08 0508 out and back from Craigentinny, North Berwick being visited at 0630 with 37606 and 611 in charge. While the driver was changing ends, I whipped out to get this photo; there was no time to waste if we weren't to delay the early commuters. 5 July 2008.

being cleared for its next use. After an overnight stay in the Ramada Plaza nearby (nice rooms, expensive food!), I strolled down to the station and then took a last look at Bath Road depot. They were busy breaking up the old concrete and I noted the pit of a small turntable alongside the single track running down to St Philip's Marsh.

The requested start time of 1800 materialised in the final timings as 1630 so the three of us, myself, Rob Clamp and Craig Tonkin, began prepping the coach at 1500. A Serco driver had already started up (and brake-tested) the locos, smoking out the station environs in the process (nice of him). He departed the scene to be relieved by our driver for the week, Richard Sargent, who I knew from my time working on Pandora. The first bit of recording we had to do was the Filton–Patchway avoider, this presenting us with our first difficulty compared with TRU, namely that we were running blind in both directions with just the big yellow nose of a locomotive to see out of the end windows. There was also the problem that the driver could only be contacted by radio, which was often subject to interference from taxi firms when running in urban areas. However, it was a nice evening and our progress westward seemed to be being closely monitored by local enthusiasts. We thundered up out of the Severn

Tunnel, already ahead of schedule (hardly surprising with 3,500 horsepower on tap for a single vehicle) and were made to wait in the loop at Ebbw Jn. Across the tracks beside us I could see the remains of another closed depot and was reminded of the days when you could expect to see lines of Class 37s, here and elsewhere, waiting to haul coal and steel traffic. I suspected that we probably had the only 37s working in South Wales that day!

The next bit of recording was from Radyr Branch Junction, round the back of Canton DMU depot and up to Radyr itself. This used to be another loco number collecting port of call for me but now the yard there is a housing estate. We returned to Cardiff in order to approach Radyr once more, this time from the Queen St direction, only to get confused over which line we had to record; the up main goes round the outside of Radyr platform and we requested the wrong one. Never mind, we collected a reportable fault in the process so maybe it wasn't such a bad call …

The RST we were using was set up for Cardiff to Merthyr but the timings had us going to Tower Colliery first. That meant having to stop the train at Pontypridd in order to load a different RST into the TGC. By this time, the local track engineer had joined us in anticipation of seeing some work created for him; I found it a little strange, though as I was under the impression that Tower Colliery had closed. Oh well, we were held in Stormstown loop for nearly an hour before finally getting the go-ahead and understandably with a degree of trepidation – the driver told us that the last run up there had produced several 'close the line' faults. Sure enough, once past Aberdare the fault printer started chattering away in earnest and within 4 miles we had accumulated twelve 'thirty-six-hour' faults and two 'close the lines'! If there was a title of worst stretch of line in Britain (the antithesis of the prize lengths of old?), this would be a contender, no mistake. The poor old printer seemed overwhelmed by the sudden burst of activity and promptly jammed! However, with the track engineer's permission, I was careful to wait until we'd returned safely back south of Aberdare before I called the signaller with the detail of the most severe faults. With no immediate prospect of other traffic using the line, it would have been silly to trap ourselves on the wrong side of them while they were checked, losing time in the process and jeopardising the chance to do the rest of our night's work.

An illustration of how we got messed around on these trips sometimes, came with a phone call to say that due to a possession we weren't going up to Treherbert. Then ten minutes later there was another call saying that the possession had been cancelled for our benefit!

Anyway, both that run and the one before it to Merthyr were a bit of an anticlimax (thank goodness, following the Tower Colliery trip) but it still proved to be a long night. Some of the hardier enthusiasts had been out with their tripods in places but even they had disappeared by the time we called at Treherbert in the early hours. We finally ended up stabling at Canton depot around 0300, where the yard staff hadn't been expecting us. 'May you live in interesting times,' did I hear someone say?

The curtains in my hotel room at the Angel were good but not good enough to stop me waking at 0830, so I only got a few hours' sleep. I wasn't going to pass up a breakfast though and it was surprisingly good for a change. Wednesday night's shift was going to be shorter (hopefully), but only by an hour or so. Although the original plan had us doing all the branches in South Wales, a few hadn't made it into the timings – Maesteg, Barry Island, Penarth and Ebbw Vale would have to wait for the next visit of TRU. First up was the freight-only route to Cwm Bargoed; another line that only seemed to entertain track recording trains and enthusiast specials back then! Incredibly, in contrast to the Tower branch, we found zero reportable faults on the way out. So when we reached the end of the line at that rather isolated spot, we could relax and take the opportunity to breathe in the air as night fell over the Welsh hills. It couldn't last. The fun started once more on return to Ystrad Mynach, where the signalman found the points for the branch wouldn't budge and we were stuck watching the service trains go by as we

Before it was fitted with ETCS, 97301 stood in when there was a shortage of Class 31s at Derby. It is shown waiting at St Blazey while 66169 clears the Newquay branch on a china clay working. 8 June 2011.

In place of TRU, this formation of TIC and 9701 powered by 97301, made a tour of the South West and included a working visit to the West Somerset Railway. Having been to Minehead, the train calls at Blue Anchor, where the crew had a break for ice creams. It went on to spend the weekend at Bishops Lydeard for the duration of that summer's diesel gala. I wonder if somebody there took a shine to TIC, as when it retired from NR service it was sent to the WSR for restoration at Williton. 9 June 2011.

awaited the arrival of a maintenance crew to sort it out. I was left wondering how we got on to the branch in the first place as it was basically the same pointwork! The enforced delay meant we weren't going to Rhymney afterwards – Bargoed box shut at 2345 and there was no way we could get back in time for that. No question of asking the man to do a spot of overtime for us, then?

Well, at least that meant we were ahead of time now as we ran down towards Cardiff Bay. I'd never been there before and couldn't resist stepping on to the platform; I wondered where our spectators were this time? Then it was back north to another new bit of territory for me, Coryton. This is a peculiar place, squeezed as it is between peoples' back gardens in an outer suburb of the city. If there was ever a goods yard here, it has long disappeared beneath housing. No sign of a car park either. Running back to Canton, a short stop was made in Cardiff station to hand over our printouts to the local maintenance man and then it was a taxi ride back to the hotel.

The last night on this little tour was the longest (groan). To begin with, we traversed the line to Machen Quarry and then made a number of manoeuvres at Park Junction in the fading light. That lost us time but slack in the schedule

came to our rescue. The hardest part now was the boredom factor as we were just recording loops to Hereford and back and then a few more between Filton Junction and Bromsgrove. In that situation, you had little to do but you daren't take your mind off the job entirely as you might not notice when you were getting close to the next piece of recording; a sudden message over the radio from the driver, asking whether we needed to go into a certain loop (as stated on the timings) would likely bring you to your senses! As before, our two 37s made a lovely sound reverberating in the Severn Tunnel, then once more going up the Lickey Bank at some (by now) unearthly hour. Back at Derby, all our onboard equipment was shut down ready for a quick getaway the moment we pulled into the RTC yard. I took the remaining recorded CDs and printed sheets into the office and completed my timesheet there, too. Dawn was breaking as the taxi took me home. Thank God I didn't have to do this too often, I thought.

Working on NMT most of the time, I suppose I tended to pass through the north of England on monitoring trains at speed, whether it was along the ECML, WCML or over the scenic Settle and Carlisle. The odd shift change would take place at Leeds as a prelude to an occasional late evening run over the Pennines, but by and large the only overnight stops would be in Newcastle. Even with the loss of much mining and industrial activity, there were still plenty of freight-only lines and curves to be covered in Yorkshire, Humberside and Tyneside. These were usually tackled in weekly chunks by the TRU, or the TIC, if TRU was unavailable … and I must say that wasn't the nicest place to be in hot or cold weather.

After travelling in to Derby from home late the previous night, 0430 on a freezing and snowy 29 November 2010 found me in the RTC yard trying to start the generator on TIC (formed up with 31465 and a DBS). I wanted to get it running in plenty of time before departure at 0600 so that the coach might be fairly warm from the start as I knew from bitter experience that, with holes in its floor, the draughts would soon be keeping the temperature down. It wasn't easy; being several degrees below zero, I suspected the diesel fuel wasn't as fluid as it ought to be (possibly not the right sort anyway for winter) as the engine would fire but not run for very long. The moment you tried to put a load on it, it would cut out but after several goes it eventually improved and then I found that only by putting the kettle on at the same time as all the heaters would it lead to cutting out again. The pipes were frozen, of course, and started to leak too as the day wore on! Doing the washing up proved awkward as well.

Anyway, after my colleague Dan Purvis had arrived, our driver Ian Thurman took us to Sheffield where we picked up our third team member, Phil McDermott.

After a relatively uneventful shift, we were in Doncaster on the Monday night and only heard that Tuesday's shift was cancelled once we'd got to the train (early) in the West Yard. Phil lived locally so kindly drove us to his house for a much-needed bite to eat and somewhere to sit in the warm while we waited for further news. Our main driver for that day had been borrowed for snowplough duties, as it transpired! The TIC itself could only be moved unproductively to Darlington, which was where we met it the next day (early again) after a hair-raising taxi ride in the snow from our hotel in Middlesbrough. Yes, I firmly believe that taxi rides were actually the most dangerous part of our job!

Arriving at Darlington station, we found the main line covered in six inches of snow but we couldn't assume nothing would come charging southwards at line speed, so a call to the signaller was required to allow us to cross in safety (not forgetting to confirm when we were across, of course). TIC was parked in the small yard north of the station (which I'd not seen another vehicle use before or since). All our equipment started OK but the driver (Jason Rogers) couldn't move the train more than a few yards before the brakes came on – water had frozen in the pipes and we weren't going to move until the system had warmed

It's 0440 and clearly the instruction has been given to leave these two Class 31s ticking over in the RTC yard overnight, in the hope of avoiding any starting problems or issues with frozen pipes come departure time; it was around -8 degrees, so that was a wise judgement to make. No. 31465 will power my train (TIC), due to depart around 0630, while No. 31602 is coupled to a UTU set. 29 November 2010.

The driver has told me that we will be waiting at Sheffield for a few minutes, so while he has gone to the DBS to make another brew, I've whipped out my camera and tripod to record the scene. The formation hauled by 31465 is 999508, 6264 and 9714. 29 November 2010.

through. Thank goodness there was a DBS in the formation; that was a lot warmer inside than TIC would ever be, so we decamped to there (with the milk!) to sip hot coffee and eat whatever food we had until the formation could be moved. After a couple of hours we left, but the recording programme was cut short by frozen points in various places and the lack of any staff available to free them. There was also so much lying snow that the rubber shrouds around the Optel system were acting like a snowplough in one direction and a scoop in the other, leading to the formation of one great mass of ice under the vehicle that was interfering with the lasers. When the safe opportunity arose we got out to try and clear the worst of it, but it was a losing battle. Proceeding to Tees Yard, we summoned a taxi for a shorter ride back to the hotel and a much-needed proper meal.

It was almost a repeat performance the next day: fresh overnight snowfall, up too early for the hotel breakfast and a dodgy taxi ride – this time our man drove into the deep stuff on the way into the yard itself and we were obliged to push him out. Wading through the drifts across this half-abandoned yard wasn't exactly fun either, as you could never be sure whether you were about to step into a hole. On reaching the train, one driver was already there with the bad news: 'Didn't they tell you? We're starting two hours late because Jason's been called in for snowplough duties again!' I rang Control to confirm this, only to hear the

rather pathetic excuse of, 'I didn't call as I didn't want to disturb you.' Hmm, we could have got our breakfast if you had, I thought … thanks for that! Ever heard of voicemail? In the event, it was decided that our presence on the network there wouldn't be welcome anyway so we just waited until a path was free for a straight run back to Derby. Not being required to do any track recording meant we could sit in the constant warmth of the DBS, rather than the steadily chilling environment of TIC. No. 31465 led us all the way home and it was fun to sit in the DBS's cab to watch the clouds of powdered snow trailing in our wake. Back at Derby, the train went straight into the EDU to thaw out. Ken Keegan (the duty shunter) said he'd never seen so much snow on the underside of a train and I reckon there must have been at least two tons of it there; when I looked in the next day, the pit was deep in melt water and the workshop floor covered in large puddles.

TIC was to survive a few more stays of execution before it was displaced by TIC2 (the former Track Lab Mark 2 977974, that had seen use in the original NMT formation). Shorn of its recording gear, it sat in the RTC yard for a time as most retiring test train vehicles did before they were finally disposed of, later being sold to the West Somerset Railway for a new life as an inspection saloon coach. I look forward to seeing it running in its old guise again.

The sun shines on a snowy Tees Yard, though I'm about to beat a hasty retreat into the warmth of that DBS coach as the next blizzard is clearly coming. No. 31465 is about to take us straight back to Derby, our work curtailed for the rest of that week. 2 December 2010.

Ready to roll: Phil McDermott has the all-important bottle of milk as he, Dan Purvis and I leave DBS 9714 for the colder confines of TIC. We'd been waiting for the brake pipes in the train to thaw out before the train could leave the sidings at Darlington. 1 December 2010.

Above: Here comes that snow, although Jason Rogers still has his pre-departure checks to complete before we are good to go back to Derby. 2 December 2010.

Left: The laser hazard warning seems somewhat redundant owing to the great mass of snow that has collected on the measuring bogie of TIC, seen at Tees Yard. 2 December 2010.

TIC traverses the single-track viaduct that takes the up and down Bletchley Chord line across Saxon Way; when the east–west route comes into its own, perhaps they'll need another bridge here! DRS locos providing the power are 37607 and 37604. If the train had come a few moments later, I suppose I could have taken a nice photo of a Scania truck instead. 8 July 2011.

By 2011, the Cambrian lines had gone over to ETCS Level 2 signalling, which meant that we had to use 97/3s with TIC instead of the TRU. However, a problem with the speedo on 97302 manifested itself and we were to proceed no further than Tywyn on this visit. Together with 97304, the ensemble is seen in the up relief siding there waiting for a RVEL fitter to drive from Derby to fix it. 11 January 2011.

Radio Survey Coach

Apart from one night spent aboard the old two-car DMU *Iris II* when I had my training with Serco in 2002, I hadn't been involved with the radio survey side of operations at all. In the summer of 2009 however, I was rostered for a few weeks aboard an RSC train, beginning in the south London area and monitoring the CSR (Cab Secure Radio) frequencies. There were two Mark 2 RSC coaches: RSC1 was 977868 and RSC2 was 977869, the latter being different in that it carried its own generator and could work alone. At this time, however, both were coupled together with power being taken from the generator in the DBS (usually 9701); the RSC vehicle nearest the loco acted as a barrier vehicle for the crew's benefit, due to the excessive fumes from NR's Class 31s being drawn into the air-con.

The RSC coaches were used to check the strength of radio signals from lineside aerials where CSR, NRN

Tywyn is the location again with a very early morning shot there of 31285 with the RSC set, mid-summer but not especially warm I recall. Our stabling on the Cambrian was normally at Machynlleth, but there was a story of a test train needing to overnight in the siding at Pwllheli once. Before shunting into it, a key was required to unlock the points, not obtainable from rail staff but from a lady who had a shop nearby. The crew were advised to keep the key until their departure, as it couldn't be guaranteed that the lady concerned would open her door early the following morning! 26 June 2009.

RSC3 (977997) is the second vehicle behind 9481 and 37602 in the sole remaining siding at Aberystwyth (37218 is at the rear, with two further unrecorded brake force vehicles). The testing carried out by this train was a prelude to introduction of ETCS on the Cambrian lines. 19 August 2009.

(National Radio Network) and RETB (Radio Electronic Token Block) were used. Each crew that manned them had to remember to pick up the yellow 'boxes of tricks' from the office in Derby prior to each tour of surveying. These were the heavy plastic cases carrying the testing equipment that needed to be plugged into the aerials mounted on the roof of the coaches. Resources seemed to be concentrating on testing the next technology GSMR (Global System for Mobiles – Rail) that would render the NRN and CSR systems redundant, so with GSMR testing about to be stepped up, a third Mark 2 coach RSC3 (977997) was in preparation.

CSR testing involved the support of two or three men in road vans who would go to the base stations (fixed aerials on the ground) that we had to test and physically 'key' these up for us for about twenty minutes at a time. We would phone them as we approached their area of coverage, monitor and record the varying signal strengths we detected and then call them once again (as the train pulled away) to ask them to 'de-key'. The support company didn't always have enough staff to achieve all the testing laid down in the plan. That sometimes meant that some poor soul would have to operate one base station before jumping in the van again to drive quickly to another in time to key that one up for us. It didn't always happen and the van was sometimes still caught in traffic while the train passed by the aerial – that went down as lost testing!

Later on, a remote keying device was installed on the train for us to do the keying for ourselves; on the face of it, that should have made things easier but in practice the process was rather convoluted and not helped by the fact that the device was set up to 'de-key' itself after only fifteen minutes. This meant that you had to keep an eye on your watch, as well as the signal strengths showing on the laptop, in case the train was unable to pass through the monitoring area quickly enough.

CSR tended to be used mostly in the larger conurbations, so RSC testing often meant working shifts in the London or Glasgow areas, punctuated by the odd foray to the wilds of RETB operation, namely north Scotland and (at the time) the Cambrian line or east Suffolk. I never got to do any shifts that checked NRN.

I had just the one experience of RETB testing in Wales, scheduled over two nights. You would think that would be ample time for Shrewsbury to Pwllheli and Aberystwyth but problems with our loco (31285) meant we only just completed the work required. The set had made a transit move from Derby during one day whilst the staff travelled to meet it by service train on the next, ready to work overnight. To perform the testing, we needed the line to ourselves and would have to wait until all service trains had finished and returned to depot before we could then leave Machynlleth just after midnight. There was some doubt initially as to whether the testing would take place as the support company was having particular trouble staffing its vans. In the event, it called in people from the south of England, who then had to drive up to Wales and find base stations that they'd never been to before in the dark. No pressure, huh? One poor chap who rang in didn't seem to have any directions for his base station and we only had its name to go on, namely Mynydd Rhiw. Using our internet access in the coach, I fruitlessly searched the online Ordnance Survey map extracts (thinking it would be close to the line). A Google search then suggested a location some way out on the Lleyn peninsular and sure enough, there it was – an aerial on a 1,000ft mountain top, about 10 miles west of the end of the line at Pwllheli! With some difficulty we gave our man directions over the phone and he found it eventually, just him in his van in the middle of far-flung Wales in the early hours of the morning. I didn't envy him; at least I was safe and snug in my train, sipping hot coffee and munching M&S cookies.

I was a little disappointed that the RETB testing that I was rostered for in the far north had got cancelled as it would have been nice to (maybe) see the dawn breaking up there. The only work in Scotland I ended up with would be in the Glasgow area – with all due respect, not quite as pleasant.

A return to the Cambrian was on the cards, though as the first wave of GSMR testing began using the new RSC3; it fell to me to work it from 17–21 August. I was a bit concerned for two reasons: firstly I'd not yet set foot upon the vehicle, and secondly, it was fresh out of the EDU and had only gone out for one main-line test run the previous Friday! Experience had taught me to expect problems and there were some, but no real show-stoppers. We seemed to have crockery and cutlery; stores (drinking water, paper towels, cleaning fluids, etc) were also supposed to have been loaded aboard. Sure, they had been (as I was told after we were under way) but into the brake vehicle coupled next to it and the gangway doors between the two were firmly bolted! I later discovered that the rest of the train's external doors (there were another two Mark 2s added for brake force) were all unlocked, with one droplight window open – very inviting for any unwitting passenger who thought we might be their expected train, should we pull into a platform. Another irritation was the position of the smoke alarms in the vestibules, right in the middle of the ceiling so that by the end of the week I must have banged my head on them about twenty times.

The first run was down to Didcot to pick up the London-based GSMR testing staff who were trained in how to assess the newly installed system. Once running at

The working desk inside coach RSC1, showing two yellow 'boxes of tricks' set up and wired up to the antennae on the roof of the vehicle. I suspect those chairs may have been ex-BR drivers' seats!

speed, it was good to note that RSC3 was a quieter ride than the other two RSC vehicles, although it was a pity the generator compartment door wasn't a better fit. Fixing that detail would have made it very pleasant. Monday's testing involved a number of runs through the Severn Tunnel between Bristol and Newport, stabling overnight in Temple Meads station. The locos required fuelling at Barton Hill depot first and the driver, Dave Pond, asked me to ride in the cab of 37608 back to the station to assist with shunting. This served to remind me that, despite the hum from our generator it was still quieter to be in the train than on the loco.

That night, I checked in at the Holiday Inn Express hotel: 'Have you a car, sir?' asked the receptionist (with parking in mind). 'No … I've got a train … but I parked it at the station.' That brought a smile. 'Cool!' he said.

Next morning, after breakfast over at Wetherspoons on Temple Gate, the testing around the Severn Estuary resumed, together with a somewhat curiously timetabled pair of visits to the Machen Quarry branch at the end! Enquiries with our testers could reveal no purpose for these and indeed they decided to alight at Newport before that and go home, leaving me to make a joint decision with the drivers (Richard Sargent and Jason Dicks) and Serco Control about what to do with the time. As Jason needed to refresh his route knowledge of the line, we decided to make one run up there and then sit out by Cardiff Canton in the up

loop before resuming our booked path. This resulted in me having my own personal railtour up the branch with top and tailed Class 37s, duly recorded photographically at Machen. A long trek north to Aberystwyth then ensued with a single tester collected at Shrewsbury to monitor signal strengths between there and Machynlleth (Mac, for short). Our having to stable the train out at Aber was due to the fact that the Cambrian summer-timetabled steam train was occupying our favoured siding for test trains at Mac, which resulted in me walking through the streets of the seaside town at 0115 and hoping that the Richmond Hotel proprietor would still be around to let me in (as I had earlier been assured he would!). All was fine and I woke the next day to admire a pleasant seafront view and then enjoy an excellent cooked breakfast. I recall wishing that it could always be like that.

That Wednesday was a free day as my late finish the night before meant I couldn't possibly work again for the 0530 run to Pwllheli. I did buy a ticket to Dovey Junction though to meet them on the return. With their testing complete, Craig Merry and the testers got off at Mac and I rode back to Aber on RSC3 with drivers Jason Rogers and Alan Guest up front – another personal railtour.

Thursday was a repeat of Wednesday's testing (so with the 0530 start no repeat of the nice breakfast, sadly) but it was worth it just to enjoy the views on the run up the coast to Pwllheli. The testers weren't entirely happy with

No. 37602 has reached Machen Quarry with RSC3. It was never established why the train had to come here!
18 August 2009.

DRS-liveried 37218 brings the Radio Survey train off the Cambrian at Sutton Bridge Jn, Shrewsbury and passes Network Rail-owned 97302 and 304 on Coleham shed. It was a case of 'over to you, boys' as only the 97/3s were allowed to run trains to Aberystwyth and Pwllheli from not long after this date. 20 August 2009.

the results they were getting, which meant the train would be back in the vicinity again before too long, I suspected. We passed the (now much-missed) steam service headed by No. 76079 at Harlech on our return mid-morning and then sat on Mac depot for a time, hoping there might be a chance of an earlier path through to Shrewsbury. No such luck. Drivers were changed again at Shrewsbury so it was Richard Sargent who drove me (personal railtour number three) down the Welsh Marches route to Bristol. I knew at the time that work would rarely be as pleasurable as this again! Another series of tests around Bristol, Chepstow and Newport were the order of the day for Friday before the last of the testers departed back to London (and hopefully now remembering to have their hi-viz vests with them at ALL times, as they had walked down a siding to board the train at Bristol on the Tuesday without wearing them!).

Then with work completed, it was personal railtour number four back to Derby via the Lickey. The driver kindly invited me up front to ride in the cab again but I thought on this occasion it might be wiser to stay in the train. Besides, I needed to keep an eye on our desktop PC to check the cricket score; it was the final Ashes Test that England had to win that summer and as we headed

homeward, Stuart Broad was busy taking Aussie wickets and I was able to pass on the good news of each one to the driver on the two-way radio.

I wouldn't wish to give the impression that being an OTT was easy, though. The comment I read in one of the magazines about it being 'nice work if you can get it' (referring to the kind of loco-haulage one experienced over various routes) was understandable but rather wide of the mark. Yes, there were instances like those that I've just described but plenty of uncomfortable times, too. And when things did start to go wrong, you were expected to take the appropriate action in the interests of all. As with driving the train, it was in times of crisis that you earned your wages.

It had been one of the most enjoyable weeks I'd had on any train I think, but there was to be no more radio survey work for me. No sooner had I become familiar with the equipment (and been assessed as competent on it), the schedules all got changed and I wasn't rostered on the RSCs again. Today, GSMR is operational across the country and radio survey work is conducted in parallel with other testing so no RSC-specific trains are required anymore. And all trains on the Cambrian lines now have to be hauled by one of the four ETCS-fitted Class 97/3s.

RSC3 is in this formation, seen powering away from Reading on to the Berks & Hants with 37604 and 37038 clearly unified in effort. Gary Payne is the driver. 30 November 2011.

Another view for the history books as Didcot 'A' Power Station ceased generating soon after this. I feel a certain attachment to the place, having observed the MGR trains feeding it from the Midlands coalfield on a daily basis when I was young. Nos 37604 and 038 await resumption of testing for GSMR in the Thames Valley. 2 December 2011.

Driver Colin Hayward is in the cab of 9701 as RSC1 passes the four chimneys at Stewartby on the Marston Vale line. 16 January 2012.

To be working a train that stopped at places for a while in pleasant weather was something of a rare treat; turnarounds at termini like this one at Largs were usually done quickly. However, on this occasion the rest of my team have had time to wander off and the driver is probably enjoying his lunch in the DBS. No. 31602 *Driver Dave Green* has been shut down to spare the locals from its fumes. 7 July 2009.

Nos 37425 and 37667 top and tail a working of RSC1 (977868) when it was being accompanied by Mentor to provide a generator and messing facilities. The train was touring a number of lines in South Wales as part of the GSMR roll-out and had just made a reversal at Pantyffynnon. 22 May 2014.

Scenes from the RTC

Outside RVEL's maintenance shed at the RTC we have 73138, 31465 and 73139. 13 June 2011.

Two staff members kitted out in hi-viz gear walk out from the Engineering Development Unit (EDU) framed by the NMT, SGT, 97301 and 31459. 12 May 2011.

Above: I must include this shot of the RTC shunter as the staff were clearly quite attached to it. They knew that Serco's involvement was coming to an end but were determined to provide the loco with a suitable livery before things changed. No. 08417 is quietly ticking over, waiting for the next call to duty; look at those buffers! 23 February 2010.

Opposite top: No. 97302 is parked outside the doors of the EDU early on a winter's morning. 5 December 2011.

Opposite bottom: Very early in the morning inside the EDU, somebody has kindly left the lights on so I've managed to obtain this view of 97304 *John Tiley* in the middle of an examination. Getting photos in here wasn't easy as each of the roads was often fully occupied with vehicles receiving attention of some sort. NMT awaits me outside and by that afternoon I shall be in Ayr. 15 November 2011.

Above: No. 97303 (formerly 37178) pauses during an extensive shunting session in the RTC yard at Derby. The large ETCS transponder (supplied by Ansaldo) can just be seen slung underneath the loco between the front bogie and the fuel tank. If the track looks a little uncared for, I would just say that derailments were by no means unknown here. 25 June 2010.

Opposite top: Nos 97302, 31105, 31602 and 43014 are present in the RTC yard. The number of trains parked up is probably greater than normal due to operations being affected by the weather. 3 December 2010.

Opposite bottom: A gathering of Class 31s at the front of the 'dirty' shed at the RTC, its oil-stained apron reminiscent of those BR diesel depots of the past. Nos 31105, 31285 (with 31459 behind) and 31452 are on show – bonus points if you spotted D1015 *Western Champion* in the background, visiting the EDU for weighing. 25 July 2009.

Above: TRU moves up to the ground signal controlling exit from the RTC yard. A second exit was close to the signal box at the end of Way & Works sidings. 25 August 2011.

Opposite top: It's Serco livery now a memory, No. 08417 manoeuvres the NMT around the yard on a sunny June afternoon. 3 June 2011.

Opposite bottom: No 43062 *John Armitt* peeps out from the back of the EDU at the RTC. The building in the left background is the staff canteen; always a good place to meet up with former colleagues and catch up on the gossip! 23 July 2009.

Structure Gauging Train
(or 'The One with the Strange Wagon')

I'd largely managed to escape working the SGT ever since I started my job, apart from a couple of familiarisation trips back in 2002–03. As its white light system required complete darkness in which to record successfully, it tended to work night shifts and not go out at all during the summer months. So I was never inclined to ask to work it at any time! I could handle night work on occasion but always preferred day shifts. Anyhow, another new roster plan was produced in May 2010 and SGT duly appeared in my column: a few shifts that would be just enough to remind me what it did, but not really enough to properly teach me how to do it sufficiently for me to assume the task of lead OTT.

The added spice to the mix was that SGT had recently been combined with UTU4, partly as a means to reduce test train paths (and costs) and partly to obtain as much gauging data as possible, due to there being a paucity in the amount that the ORR then required Network Rail to have produced in

that area of asset management. As with most of the other monitoring trains, the main strength of the SGT is its ability to acquire data in large quantities and reduce the requirement to send people out on to the track to carry out manual surveys. Gauging is all about assessing the infrastructure for the size and shape of the space envelope that is available for trains to pass through safely. It's important to appreciate that while platform edges, bridge arches, tunnels and retaining walls are fixed (by and large!); the track alongside them has a tendency to move. It can move under the influence of traffic, the effect of rainwater and moisture on the formation and, of course, the occasional realignment effected by reballasting and tamping. Data from the SGT feeds into the National Gauging Database, which over the years has acquired an increasing importance in the safe running of trains, particularly as both freight and passenger rolling stock seems to have got ever wider and longer in a bid to maximise loadings.

Graham Wildgoose updates his log inside the control vehicle of SGT (975081). I'd never seen that kind of industrial arrangement of PCs before; it certainly avoided the sort of issues, such as shifting keyboards and juddering screens that were seen on other monitoring trains. The big red emergency stop button shut down all the lights and cameras on the gauging wagon. 12 May 2010.

Still gleaming in its recently applied yellow livery, 31285 stables in Exeter Riverside Yard with the SGT rake prior to a night shift on the Devon main line. This was my first proper shift away from working the NMT and we were expecting to finish in Bristol, where I had a hotel room booked. In the event, things didn't go to plan and we ended up returning to Exeter, leaving me to catch the first service train at around 0530. As it was an all-stations stopper, I didn't reach the hotel in Bristol until about eight o'clock, when the receptionist received me with a disapproval that suggested he thought I'd been out on the town all night! 14 November 2003.

A long train formation of seven vehicles, top and tailed by 31233 and 285, straddled the RTC yard one Monday evening as I walked up to it with experienced SGT technician, Graham Wildgoose. It had been his train since way back but he'd been off it for a while and like me was also wondering what we'd find when we got onboard. DC460000, the special wagon with the slot in it for the white light system, had been upgraded with a new Laserflex system mounted externally on one end. This took the form of a black cylinder about the size of a dustbin (hence its nickname 'Dusty Bin') with a ring of lasers and small cameras around it. The standing instruction was to operate both old and new systems together but a fault with the old system meant this time we'd only be running Laserflex. SGT had its own DBS vehicle, 9708, with cameras and infrared lamps fitted. However, due to this being coupled end on with the DBS of UTU4 (9714) the only camera view would be from loco 31233. A procedure had also been written stipulating that the train in contact with Control (in this case UTU4) would take the lead so their OTT spoke to the driver on one radio channel and to us on another. It wasn't possible to walk through from one train set to the other with the DBS's coupled together as they were.

The first problem we found was that the camera feed from the loco didn't work. No. 31285 had been used the previous week but had been swapped for 233 and there was now a problem with the connectors that couldn't be solved in the time available. Consequently there was little for me to do at that point except chat to our other team member Phil Blanksby, a new colleague who I'd not met before. Departing at 2230, a quick transit move over to the WCML at Lichfield followed before UTU4 lowered its ultrasonic probes on the approach to Weaver Junction and Graham set Laserflex going. It was then a case of a steady 30mph (normal monitoring speed for a UTU) all the way to Carlisle that would take up half the night. Luckily for us, SGT still had an accommodation vehicle in the rake together with mattresses in its three sleeping berths so I got my head down for a while and watched the early morning light appear over the northern fells, feet up by the window with the heating full on – very cosy!

Looped at Tebay, a sleeper train came by us very soon after (which suggested it'd been running close behind). After that it was a case of rolling quietly down to Carlisle and into the station sidings, where all monitoring kit was shut down and drivers were changed. The OTTs walked to their hotel for a few hours' shut-eye. However, I'd already

decided I would catch the train up again at Ayr ready for the Tuesday afternoon's run over to Stranraer. For me, it was a daylight trip along that line that couldn't be missed!

After about three hours' sleep I checked out of the hotel and caught a Pendolino up to Glasgow, then a fast EMU down to Newton-on-Ayr station to walk to Falkland yard. At that time, the yard would typically host a rake of coal wagons but on this occasion there were only yellow trains: NMT on its usual six-weekly visit, a big Loram grinder unit and SGT/UTU4! Knowing that the future of the yard was in question, I made sure I got the necessary photos before boarding the UTU. In charge for that one shift was Mark Bennett, who was quite happy for me to go along for the ride. And what a pleasant ride it was; climbing up into the

Left: This is a view inside the Structure Gauging Wagon DC460000. An arch of white lights, cameras and individual cooling fans can be seen, together with 'port holes' for the crew to look out of to check the alignment of the light pattern. The video and structure measurements recorded by the train were assessed back in the office, although I believe that any clearances deemed to be dangerously close were flagged up to the onboard crew for them to assess and make a judgment as to whether to close the line to traffic.

Below: This is the workspace on the gauging wagon. I like the way that the number 0 has been used in place of a letter O in 'OPTICAL' and 'MODIFIED'! 'When it goes for scrap, I'm having that plate!,' one of the drivers told me.

No. 31285 is stabled with the SGT (consisting of 99666, 975280, 975081, DC460000 and 9708) at Aberdeen's Clayhills Depot on 20 October 2010. Running as a Class 4 train, the SGT generally recorded at speeds up to 60mph and transited at 75. Later on it tended to run in conjunction with a UTU set and consequently recorded at 30.

hills above Girvan, the yellow gorse was in bloom and the sun shone most of the way as 31233 wound its way towards the port station. This was something else with a question mark over its future at the time, with the possibility of ferry services being switched to Cairnryan and the railway perhaps truncated at Girvan, I was informed. I hoped that wouldn't happen. Stranraer signal box was being manned specially (by someone from Glasgow) for our arrival into platform 2, as the normal infrequent service trains just ran in and out of the main platform 1. While I wandered around the station area taking as many photos as I could, Mark and two others had gone off into the town and kindly rang me to see if I fancied some fish and chips. I had actually brought a microwave meal with me but the thought of them chomping chips while I ate my miserable offering was sufficient to change my mind. Cod and chips, oh yes please! We departed on time, heading back to the hills as the sun set in the west. Just as we tackled the steepest part of the climb to Glenwhilly, the infamous Swan's Neck, the rear loco, 31233, appeared to stop pushing so 465 did all the work … and not for the only time that week, it turned out. The run onwards to Polmadie seemed to take an eternity in the darkness and we parked in the secure compound on the down side of the main line.

After a proper night's sleep in Glasgow, the camera on 233 was coaxed back to life on the Wednesday evening, which meant I got to see the structure gauging process working properly at last, albeit only with a trailing view. Phil showed me how to uncover the lasers and cameras on Dusty Bin and I could see how air was blown over these to keep them clear of dirt and rainwater. On this trip to Inverness, a local technical officer joined us at Perth for a ride to Pitlochry. At least somebody was going to appreciate the work we were doing that night – because of the lack of SGT running up to that time many local teams were having to undertake extra spot surveys in possessions to get the data they needed, work that SGT was intended to relieve. Reaching Inverness at dawn, we found that the length of our train meant we had to shunt out to Millburn yard for stabling, Blue Circle siding No. 2 to be specific. The local seagulls had already mounted a guard on the train by the time we got off to wait (and hope) that our requested taxis would find us.

Although it usually meant forcing myself out of bed a few hours after arriving at a hotel, I always liked to make breakfast if I could. A bit of a novelty back then, ITV4 was available in my room so I watched one episode of *Randall & Hopkirk (Deceased)* and *The Saint* on TV (endlessly

Left: Nicknamed 'Dusty Bin' (can't think why …) this is the first Laserflex unit, as attached to one end of the gauging wagon and shown with the circular sliding covers padlocked in the working position. The lasers shone out from the slots on the left with the image of what they detected being recorded by the cameras in the windows. After operation, the narrow encircling cover slides left to cover the lasers and the wider cover goes right to cover the cameras. They are then re-padlocked. The same type of fixed coupling was used again in production when the equipment was fitted between two Mark 2 coaches.

Opposite: A view from the DBS attached to UTU4 as 31233 climbs into the Galloway Hills, en route to Stranraer. 11 May 2010.

Below: At Ayr's Falkland Yard, 31233 heads a combined formation of the SGT and UTU4 (with 31465 bringing up the rear). Also present are the NMT and a Loram Grinder C2102. The style and arrangement of infrared lamps fixed to the class 31s for structure gauging work varied quite a bit, if you compare this with other photos of them. Driver Rob McKay watches from the cab as I record the scene and soon this grand consist will be on its way to Stranraer. 11 May 2010.

repeated now, of course) before I'd digested my bacon and eggs and gone back to sleep.

Thursday night's run back south was slow at first with lots of stops here and there but the other two were letting me do the logging this time and that helped keep me awake. UTU4 wasn't required to monitor the whole distance so we picked up time with some bursts of 75mph running, only to be stopped short of our Polmadie finish by an engineering possession. How often night shifts became extended by such frustrations!

Come Friday night, the new driver, Willie Burt, had a black look on his face. It seemed that sickly 31233 had shifted tyres and to monitor the problem, we needed white paint to mark the wheels. We had none but I found a bottle of Tippex in the kitchen cupboard (cunningly hidden by someone, perhaps?) and that did the job just as well. We ran out to Barassie yard (on the stump of the former Troon avoiding line) and examined them again. Sure enough, they were showing signs of movement. We couldn't risk any high-speed running on the WCML with that hindrance so the decision was taken to go on to Kilmarnock and deposit the ailing loco there, for 465 to carry on solo back to Derby. With no loco cameras to use, that meant no more gauging work that night. Fortunately, 465 seemed to be in good order as I exchanged waves with the staff in Carlisle box, the loco happily slogging its way up to Shap with 4Q15 in tow at 35mph. I had little to do then except make some notes on the week's running.

I got off at Crewe, reaching home in Hertfordshire at about 10:45. Weekends were largely spent catching up on lost shut-eye after those kinds of working weeks!

By October 2010, the decision had been taken to move the staff back to working specific train pools. That meant one group for working the NMT, one for the Radio Survey vehicles/Mentor/Track Recording and one just for the UTUs and SGT. I knew I'd be going back to the NMT so my SGT shifts that autumn would very likely be my last. Working on its own again now, SGT recorded at up to 50mph so was a little less tied to working at night than the UTUs. Although the new Laserflex system didn't require absolute darkness in the way that the original white light system did, there was still no point in running before 1700hrs and the decision hadn't yet been taken to decommission white light – Laserflex was still a tad temperamental. Just to outline my role during the running of the train: I knew how to power up all the equipment but I always worked with an OTT more experienced in SGT operation, simply because they were more capable of sorting out technical problems. I had the lesser role of loading VHS tapes and logging the passing times of stations and landmarks that would help the office staff in checking and filing the data. The others thought this rather boring but I found it did no harm to my route knowledge.

My penultimate shift was probably my most eventful. We'd stabled in those up sidings north of Darlington station again in a very dark spot. Getting to or from this was

At Old Oak Common, driver Colin Hayward gets to work on the nose-end grime of DBS 9708. At the time, this was the only one of these vehicles fitted with the infrared lamps to accompany the SGT set. It also had an additional central windscreen wiper for the sake of the internally mounted camera. 14 October 2010.

awkward, what with no clear walking route in a location unfamiliar to us and a need to cross the main lines – no problem at midnight when there are few trains about but tricky walking back the next evening when there might be something approaching at 125mph! Anyway, the schedule was to run up the Bishop Auckland branch, down to Eaglescliffe and back, then home to Derby around 0430. Getting to Bishop Auckland wasn't a problem but on our return we came to a halt at Heighington as the signal lights were out. Permission was obtained from the signalman there to go over the level crossing but no further. The barriers were in emergency mode, which meant they couldn't be raised for road traffic to cross and we had to wait for a pilotman to come out to clip all the necessary points back to Darlington before accompanying our driver over that section. As the last passenger service had run that evening, we weren't expecting all this to happen too quickly! The driver (Jason Rogers) went to speak to the signalman. My colleague (Paul Walters) and I could see what was going on using the infrared camera feed from the loco (31285) and noticed that he was going out to speak to car drivers to tell them the situation. We weren't doing anything so went out to help. Eventually a local team of technicians came to investigate the fault but, in the

absence of anyone else to do it, we carried on directing the traffic. I was just relieved that most car drivers were locals who seemed to know an alternative route so we didn't have any awkward questions to answer. Eventually the pilotman arrived and we went on our way but the run to Eaglescliffe was abandoned. Straight back to Derby we went, where I was able to jump on the 0455 to St Pancras and head for home.

The final shift I did was an out and back from Derby, monitoring from Lincoln to Peterborough. Taking my boots off and getting my head down in one of the berths on the transit run back from there, my feet in a sleeping compartment window of 975280 (once known as 'Test Coach Mercury') again attracted some puzzled stares from the platform!

Today, there is no longer a specific Structure Gauging Train; the current Mark 2 SGT vehicles always run in harness with a UTU set. The strange wagon DC460000 went to Sims Metals at Beeston for scrap some time ago. I was also sorry to learn that Graham Wildgoose (or 'The Goose', as we affectionately called him) passed away in 2017. He was a key man for Serco and Network Rail, working all those night shifts as he did on the SGT for many years.

Propelled by 31285, the Structure Gauging Train makes a rare daylight transfer move along the Midland Main Line, seen here switching from the up fast to the up slow at Sharnbrook Junction. There would probably only be a driver onboard at this point, the on-train staff travelling out to meet the train at the start of its working shift that night, together with a fresh driver. The extra black paint evident on that and the control coach was intended to reduce reflections that could affect the images recorded by the cameras in the gauging wagon. 12 December 2011.

At 2100 on a Wednesday evening, the SGT had originated at Bletchley and was due to make a reversal in Tring's reversible platform 4, an unusual move in itself. However, the points at the north end of the station weren't allowing that so the train had to use platform 2 instead. This is the up fast and a southbound Pendolino had to be diverted through platform 5 while all this was happening. The glow from the infrared lamps on 31233 can just be seen in the gloom as the driver waits for the OK from the on-train staff to set off again. 6 November 2012.

Tormented by Mentor

OK, perhaps I'm being a touch unkind to such a grand old vehicle with that title. But on the few occasions I had cause to work on it, the noise from the rails when travelling at speed was particularly unpleasant. As there didn't seem to be much in the way of sound-deadening material built into it, the metallic roar from steel wheel on steel rail was barely suppressed; the worst I'd experienced on any Mark 1. It can't have helped the slight degree of tinnitus I experienced in the aftermath, although I couldn't ever prove that, of course.

Anyway, to its credit Test Coach Mentor was the longest-serving vehicle in the IM fleet. A report in *Modern Railways* (April 1973) on its introduction to service in the run-up to the electrification of the WCML north of Crewe said: 'It is at present BR's only vehicle of its kind.' And for contact measurement of overhead lines in 2018, that remained the case! When I first went onboard, I don't think it had altered much since 7 May 1974 when the Queen rode in it between Preston and Glasgow to inspect the newly electrified railway (there was still a small plaque on an internal wall to mark the occasion). A single compartment with original furnishing was still in situ like a 1950s time capsule for visitors to relax in, presumably once they'd seen the technicians at work. The heart of the vehicle was the dome, where the lead technician sat and gave a running commentary on the Overhead Line Equipment (OLE) features he saw, his voice recorded on to the video tape that would be processed back at Trent

Test Coach 'Mentor' interestingly carried an all-over yellow livery while still bearing Railtrack markings for a time. It is seen in the station sidings at Derby with pantographs mounted at both ends of the coach. 23 September 2002.

Nos 31602 and 31190 wait time in the ornate surroundings of Wemyss Bay station while on duty with Mentor. I didn't mind these sorts of slow-speed, short-journey duties with the overhead monitoring coach; it was the longer distance ones on the WCML that weren't so pleasant, as explained in the text! 23 July 2008.

House. It was often Craig Tonkin carrying out this role as he had the necessary familiarity with OLE equipment, quick enough to spot features and put a name to them at 90mph before the next came along: 'mid-point anchor', 'Kings Langley neutral section', 'overlap' … etc. The lower control room where the monitoring computer was situated had a ceiling too low for the likes of me, though it was where I tended to spend much of my time writing down various items of detail that would also be of use when checking the traces showing height and stagger of the wire, together with uplift forces (necessary to keep the pantograph pressed against the underside of the contact wire) and instances of pantograph bounce. This was the noise box and in the end I borrowed the ear defenders that usually resided in the generator room to make things a little more bearable.

The motive power for formations including Mentor was almost always diesel, for obvious reasons. For a start, being based in Derby meant that you had to begin the week with two diesels, so for the sake of minimising hire charges it made sense to keep the same two all week, even if you were under the wires most of the time. Also, wherever the train might be out-stabled, it needed to be on an unwired road so that on-train staff could safely access the roof of the coach to change the batteries needed for the instrumented pantograph. I was told that this was potentially the most dangerous duty faced by the team as there was always the chance that someone (perhaps half asleep on a dark winter's morning) might absent-mindedly forget where

they were, go through the routine of putting up the ladder to attend to the batteries … only to discover perhaps that the train had been shunted overnight from the adjacent unwired road it had originally arrived on. You only had to make that mistake once.

DRS Class 37s were always on the shifts that I did. However, EWS Class 66s came on occasionally when higher-speed running wasn't necessary, though the test-train-specific drivers allocated to us (employed initially by Serco) didn't sign those, so they also required EWS drivers. Class 67s might appear for any shifts requiring 100mph speeds, such as on the WCML fasts. For certain electrified areas that were covered (such as the Glasgow suburban network), a formation of two locos top and tailing Mentor on its own was easier to operate; without any high-speed running required, this had the advantage of being able to make use of permissive working and run into a platform where a service train might already be present. There was one time when the coach was required to work into Stansted Airport and due to fire regulations in force there, electric traction was specially hired in for a couple of days' running. Nos 86101 and 87002 were used, I recall. I was interested to hear that a small group of Network Rail staff had requested to travel on Mentor at the time. This happened every now and then but, as I'd suspected, the main reason for the visit didn't seem to be so much a desire to view Mentor checking the wires but more an excuse to enjoy the rare traction. The lead OTT on duty for it told me afterwards that the visitors had been a bit of a nuisance, sometimes jumping out of

I had done three days on Mentor (with 31190 and 602) in Scotland but wasn't required on the Thursday and Friday. However, I waited at Glasgow Central to see the train appear (with Willy Burt driving) on the Thursday prior to travelling home. This shot is no longer possible as there are now two new tracks extending through that arch. 24 July 2008.

After dropping diesel on the track out of Euston, 37602 is seen waiting for the fitter beside Camden carriage sidings. My colleague, Craig Tonkin (on the right), chats to another member of Network Rail staff – those Class 321s wouldn't need to move for a while! Silverlink County was the brand name given to the outer-suburban services the operator ran at that time. 6 August 2008.

I only worked on Mentor for a couple of weeks in 2011. On slow-speed monitoring it could be operated alone between two locos but more often it ran in a rake of four coaches for braking purposes. When doing the electrified lines around the Glasgow area, no high-speed running was necessary. Nos 37069 and 37059 bring the coach into the terminus at Glasgow Central. The main requirement was to monitor the running lines, so no programme was in place to cover every platform road here. 29 March 2011.

the train without prior notice when it stopped in a platform to take their photos – who would ever do such a thing, I ask you? Not me … I always made a point of checking with the driver first!

Good communication with the driver was possibly more important with Mentor than with any other monitoring vehicle. Even if diesel traction was in use, the driver had to work his train as if it were electric. The worst-case scenario would be for the train to get put on to an unwired loop (or diverging route) at short notice. If the driver didn't tip off the crew that this was about to happen and the technician in the dome didn't have his wits about him, the pantograph might still be raised when there was no longer a wire to push against. If they were lucky, there might be some small damage to the 'pan', should it then be lowered promptly and no other structure was around to be struck. If they were unlucky, the pan could get caught in the wire as it slid off it and then cause a de-wirement as well. That meant disruption to traffic. For the train crew, either situation also meant that something of a cloud hung over them whilst an inquest was conducted to find out what had gone wrong … and who was to blame! Usual procedure was only to raise or lower the pan whilst the train was stationary, but lowering it at speed was generally a safe enough thing to do, if that proved necessary.

The only disaster I witnessed for myself on these shifts wasn't connected with the wires. We'd just pulled out of Euston early one afternoon for a burst of fast line monitoring when a strong smell of diesel began to permeate the train. Craig alerted the driver over the two-way radio and we came to a halt at the top of Camden bank adjacent to the EMU stabling sidings. Sure enough, diesel was trickling from the underside of the leading Class 37 because a fuel pipe had become detached. We probably couldn't have stopped in a more inconvenient place; our train was blocking the down fast just after the point where the two flows of long distance traffic leaving Euston came together. We had to wait for a fitter to reach us from Old Oak Common and as time wore on it was clear we were going to disrupt the beginning of that evening's rush-hour. All traffic exiting the terminus was restricted to the down slow, not only because we were there but also because the route behind us needed to be inspected and treated for the spilt fuel.

Mentor now approaches sixty-five years' service on the system, having begun life as a passenger-carrying coach in 1955. And it shows little sign of retiring yet, often being seen on non-electrified routes when it acts simply as a generator coach for the PLPR and track recording coaches that it now normally accompanies.

NMT Variety

Above: Not the brightest of pictures but it shows the scene inside DV during testing of the pantograph on the WCML. Manuals, laptops, Quail maps, empty coffee mugs, crisps and McVities ... even a lone screwdriver! The engineer staring at the pantograph on the screen also has his finger hovering over the 'Emergency Pan Down' red button, should things go awry with the contact wire interface. Plenty of moral support, too. 12 September 2006.

Opposite top: Network Rail was adamant that the NMT would only operate with power cars in its own livery, and that stipulation was adhered to. However, after it became allocated to Heaton, a Sunday test run of 43067 (once of this parish but now assigned to Grand Central) required some stock and the only spare vehicles to hand were yellow. My notes from the time provide no detail but I recall that test train driver Jason Rogers had tipped me off that he had been asked to drive this from Heaton to Doncaster and back. As luck would have it, I was staying near York and had my car to reach this location. The set is seen nudging 125 at Ryther on the Selby diversion with 43062 on the rear. 28 September 2008.

Opposite bottom: A rare visit to semaphore-signalled Lincoln for NMT as it works 1Q20, the 09.05 out and back from the RTC. The purpose of this run was to obtain 'six foot' gauging data as part of the planning for introduction of the IET and its lengthy coaching stock. 43062, with its recently attached 'John Armitt' nameplates, is at the rear as 43013 heads the train back towards Derby. August 9th 2007.

Opposite top: To carry out slow-speed testing of the geometry recording system on the newly fitted out Production Vehicle 977994, NMT was taken to the Old Dalby test track. I was due an office shift that day but asked for permission to go out and get some lineside shots of the train (I was living about 10 miles away at the time). One of the engineers based at Asfordby very kindly took me to a couple of locations as part of his duties for that day and one of them was by the original test track control centre: 43062 leads the train (slowly!) out of Grimston Tunnel, 977994 being second in the rake. I believe this was the area where the collision test with a nuclear flask took place in 1984. 7 April 2005.

Opposite bottom: A four-car NMT rake (powered by 43014/62) approaches Basingstoke with Steve Sheehan in the cab. The last coach is the spare generator vehicle 977995, easily told apart by its light grey roof. The set would visit Portsmouth Harbour later that day (with me on shift) during a series of runs designed to collect six foot gauging data on lines likely to be used in future by the IET. 19 March 2009.

Above: NMT power car 43014 passes through Sheffield on a Derby to Derby test run, after it had been fitted with a new MTU power unit in the Brush Works at Loughborough. Nos 31454 and 31459 bring up the rear to provide an extra trailing load and assist in the event of a failure. The black paint on the side of the first Mark 2 shows that it's intended for structure gauging work. Dave Talbot is driving. 7 October 2009.

Opposite top: After coming down from Heaton on the first shift, NMT sits in Ferme Park sidings before working the second one to Derby via the ECML and Leeds. Colin Campbell is the driver in the cab of 43062. 17 October 2011.

Opposite bottom: 43014 is on the blocks at Marylebone having worked 1Z16 0752 Derby RTC–Marylebone on 10 August 2011, a special run following certain track improvements on the Chiltern route. The NMT subsequently added a regular recording run here to its normal schedule, only late at night. Not long after this date, there were reports that FGW HSTs diverted from their normal terminus of Paddington qualified as first of the type to visit Marylebone. But I would say NMT came first in December 2010.

Above: This is not the best photo of the NMT that I've taken. However, it does illustrate a rare event, namely the raising of the Development Vehicle's pantograph on the main line, in this case at Wolverton during a fast line recording run to Euston. Approval to run the set with the pan raised on a routine basis wasn't granted during my time with Network Rail. 10 February 2010.

Above: Dave Smith watches from a window as NMT wends its way up into the hills on the Rylstone branch, flanges squealing as a train that was devised with main-line monitoring in mind forges a new path ... a sledgehammer to crack a nut! Just ahead can be glimpsed some golfers on the seventeenth hole of Skipton Golf Course. I played there once with my dad – who would have thought I'd return thirty years later like this? 18 July 2015.

Opposite top: So what on earth is going on here? Why has this train found its way to the end of a 9-mile-long freight-only branch in the Yorkshire Dales? Well, the track geometry data was needed (as ever!), it was noticed that the NMT had scope in its usual Saturday schedule between Derby and Heaton to do something extra and the stock was deemed gauge-cleared. So it all came together nicely. By this date, I was a fleet engineer based in Milton Keynes and I'd made a special request to join the train at Retford, not quite believing that it was going to do this but not wishing to miss out, if it did. Terry Coyne and Ian Tennant are the drivers enjoying the moment just outside the stone terminal at Rylstone. In less than ten minutes, the train had set off back to Skipton, those golfers still staring in amazement. The working was 1Q13 06.41 Derby RTC–Heaton, the power cars 43014 *The Railway Observer* and 43013 (at the far end). 18 July 2015.

Opposite bottom: It's 0500 and 43062 *John Armitt* heading the NMT has just arrived at platform 10 of St Pancras International on completion of a monitoring run over High Speed 1 for the first time. No. 43014 was at the country end. I had checked beforehand to ensure that I was OK to take any photos here, not having brought my passport with me! Note the third headlight above the cab, necessary for HS1 operation. 11 December 2010.

A Spell on TRU

The Track Recording Unit No. 950001 was a rare creature, a train that had been built from new specifically to carry out testing work for the railway – the majority of vehicles used in that regard had seen previous use as revenue-earning rolling stock. Some of my NMT colleagues had experienced shifts on this two-car unit when they joined Serco as trainee track recorders back in 2002, but I'd hardly set foot on it before the summer of 2007. Up until that time, it had been manned largely by the same two men, one of whom had been somewhat possessive of it – he'd even arranged for it to be stabled at his home town of Doncaster over some weekends, rather than be returned to Derby! It was always kept spick and span inside though, quite a home from home in fact; unlike the NMT, which came into the hands of various people from one week to the next and could never be properly equipped with useful personal items, either in the kitchen or in

TRU waits at Newtown en route to Shrewsbury. This was the second day of a tour to Wales that took in Aberystwyth, Pwllheli and then the Central Wales line. In the middle of covering the Cambrian lines, an overnight stop at the Wynnstay Arms in Machynlleth was the normal practice; it was a quirky place but with lovely food and Brains beer – a shame we were always too early off the depot to partake in their breakfast! 29 July 2008.

This is one early morning move we weren't timed to do: TRU was due to sit on the Hartlepool Power Station branch for a while but because we'd had an early start and not got any food, the driver spoke nicely to the signalman (don't they always?) and got permission for us to run into the bay at Hartlepool station. I recall we made a dash into the town to find somewhere that did bacon rolls! 27 August 2010.

the office drawers, without them being pinched now and then by light-fingered depot staff. Effectively the last of the Class 150 DMUs (having been built after unit No. 150150), TRU's operational weight was on a par with a fully laden standard 150, so its engines always had to work hard and needed plenty of TLC to keep them running reliably. Originally, its accommodation vehicle (999601) contained a stores room, a messing area and three berths so that a driver and two technicians could stay with the train. By the time I came to work on it though, nobody slept onboard anymore and the berths had been dismantled to create room for extra recording equipment. Video survey gear was also fitted to (occasionally) carry out the sort of work that I'd done in my previous role on the bubble car *Pandora*.

TRU's job was principally to record the lesser lines and the farther-flung reaches of the system and would often go out from the RTC for a week or even a fortnight at a time to record the secondary routes of Scotland or the South West, sometimes picking up the recording of certain relief lines and loops in the process. It used the tried and tested Serco-Lewis system, but you couldn't exactly step off TRC or TIC (which also used Serco-Lewis) and get stuck into work on TRU so easily. For a start, the racks of computers weren't arranged in the same way,

the filing and emailing of data was done differently and looking outside for the mileposts and the route you were taking wasn't so easy either, especially if you were running with the production vehicle (999600) trailing. Provided you were mindful of the need not to distract the driver (and not to get your fingers trapped in the hinge of the free-swinging vestibule door), with 999600 leading it was possible to nip into the cab to get a better view of where you were heading. Unfamiliarity with the routes often didn't help. Many of the lines that TRU covered only got done every six months at best, so much of the time any newcomers to the train would find themselves recording routes they'd never seen before – and quite likely in the pitch dark, too! The quaint and scenic single-track branch lines of Britain rarely have the capacity during the daytime for unusual traffic, which means TRU visits to places such as Falmouth or Windermere were invariably done early before the first service train had a chance to stake its claim to the line for the day.

Anyway, after a few forays on this unit around the freight-only lines and curves of Yorkshire (lots of short ELRs to contend with and unfathomable changes of mileage in the RSTs), a greyish out-of-season visit to 'so bracing' Skegness and an even bleaker one to Cleethorpes

Perhaps this was one location where the train team didn't mind being required to wait a while: At Port Clarence, we have reached the end of the scheduled recording and the backdrop of the Tees Transporter Bridge has made a nice frame for a photo of the unit. 27 August 2010.

(practically closed for business), I found myself heading down to Carmarthen mid-week on Wednesday, 12 December to meet the train there and Karl Garlick, my recording companion for a tour of South Wales.

That little journey took seven hours but at least the Ivy Bush Hotel in the town had improved noticeably since my previous visit on TIC when I'd been a trainee in 2003. What a shame I had to book out so early the next day! The reason for that was that we had to record the Fishguard Harbour, Milford Haven, Robeston and Pembroke Dock branches before the timetabled services got in our way. Only the Pembroke branch had a passing loop so, after a friendly word with the signalman at Clarbeston Road, we managed to slightly alter the order in which we covered these lines and ended up crossing a service train in the loop at Haverfordwest station … where there just happened to be a very nice café. I don't think I've ever eaten such a large breakfast baguette. At least we had plenty of time to digest this, though; too many meals have to be rushed when you're working on these trains.

By the time we were heading east for Swansea, a nice sunny morning was in prospect. In fact, with only the Landore East curve and a handful of loops on the main line to Cardiff remaining for us to record, we were done

by the middle of the afternoon and I had time to wander around the town for some Christmas shopping.

The following day (Friday), we'd been booked to go up to Ebbw Vale. In fact, this was supposed to have been the very day that the line was reopened to passenger traffic but that had been cancelled, unbeknown to us. With lengthy 5mph restrictions in place on the 18-mile line, it was clear we'd never manage the planned forty-eight-minute timing in either direction so permission was obtained to miss it out. The next tasks were trips to Hallen Marsh (from the Stoke Gifford direction), then Severn Beach and Portbury Dock. As there were no leaves on the trees, you could see how close these last two lines are to each other, lying as they do on opposite banks of the Avon Gorge.

We'd been running well ahead of schedule, but sooner or later somebody had to stop that kind of thing and the Bristol panel held us in Bathampton loop until we were right time again. We stabled the unit in front of Westbury box and discovered we'd been given a little gem of a hotel in the town. I couldn't remember ever having to ring a bell at a hotel entrance before, one that looked just like the front door of any other house in the street. Good food, some nice beers, a comfortable bed, clean bathroom, a powerful hot shower and a quiet location; how rarely you found all those things at the same venue!

So our Westbury stay was all too brief and after a hurried breakfast and an extended wait in the taxi outside the driver's hotel around the corner (rough night, was it, drive?) we hastened back to the train in its siding, ready for a quick getaway. However, it was apparent someone had gained illicit access to the cab overnight, probably by forcing the droplight down and unlocking the door from inside. Thankfully no damage had been done, nor had they got through the locked inner door into the recording area, which possibly meant it was only someone trying their luck. Now, I had told Control that we wouldn't be ready for the scheduled start time, as this wouldn't have given us our full twelve-hour rest. The first part of that day's recording was to collect the loops to Reading on the Berks and Hants. But what do you know? By the time we'd done all of them and without being held in any of them, we were miraculously back on schedule again! Such are the vagaries of the timings that track recording trains are given. We also had cause to close the goods loop at Theale to all traffic for a track defect, so at least we'd made ourselves useful in the process.

Then it was up to Bristol and Weston-super-Mare before a long transit move down to Laira for fuel. Clearly not wanted by the depot, the train was required to stable in a bay at Plymouth station and we retired to our hotel. Sunday was spent relaxing mostly, doing a bit of shopping and also attending to a couple of small repair jobs on the train.

Apart from the pure night shifts I did on SGT and the UTUs, without doubt one of the hardest parts of the job was heaving yourself out of bed at 'silly o'clock' in order to be in a taxi to get to the depot in reasonable time for a proper pre-departure check of the train. First things first, I found that a good hot shower was an absolute must in these circumstances – how else would you be able to wake yourself after only three or four hours' sleep? If the shower wasn't up to scratch, you were set up wrong for the day, simple as that.

Nice and early on Monday saw us heading for some unfamiliar territory in Cornwall and ending in Penzance, the first time I'd actually stayed there overnight. First though, we had to visit the rather peculiar Gunnislake branch. I say that because it involves a reversal at Bere Alston (on the old Southern main line that used to be the inland link between Exeter and Plymouth) and then a difficult climb up into the hills. As stated before, TRU was heavy with its equipment (equivalent to a full load of passengers) so it didn't take too well to these sort of lines. What also didn't help was that all trains were required to

Alongside the beach at North Blyth, TRU has reached the limit of its recording on the Alcan Import Terminal branch. In the distance can be seen the chimneys of the soon-to-close aluminium smelter and Lynemouth power station; fans of the TV detective series *Vera* may be familiar with this area! Assessment of the track into the terminal itself here was not our responsibility. 7 December 2011.

A view inside the production suite of TRU (in vehicle 999600) during a reversal at Bedlington South. The track recorder would sit at the near table with his back to the main computer rack (out of shot to the left). The left-hand screen shows the track recording traces and the right displays the log of track recording runs to be achieved with detail on start/end mileages, RST numbers and track faults. The left-hand screen at the far table shows the RTPS feed and control window for the video recorder (images displayed on the wall-mounted screen). The upper section of the curtained window housed the spot lamp for viewing mileposts in the dark. The action printer is on the right-hand side. With normally only two OTTs working this train, there was more sharing of duties required. There were occasions when my colleague would disappear to the far end of the train to make himself lunch or tea (judging it to be an opportune moment to do so), only for me to have to suddenly deal with several reportable track faults, discuss with the driver what we should be doing and make sure that the computer was still in sync. No doubt the compliment was returned at some point during the week! If the train was also passing over poor jointed track at speed, the noise and motion of the train just made it all the more interesting. Note the sheet on the far wall stating that this is 'A' (forward) end of the train. 7 December 2011.

stop at the Okeltor crossing after Calstock station before proceeding. This meant losing momentum just before the worst part of the climb, with its sharp curvature and unrelenting gradient. Several times we slowed practically to a standstill with wheels spinning until we got to a point where forward progress became impossible. Our Freightliner conductor resorted to an old trick (and one that I'm sure you wouldn't find in any manual or rule book!), namely the placing of a few lumps of ballast on the rail behind the train, which was then rolled back to crush them before restarting again, this time with just that extra bit of grip at the driver's disposal. Slowly but surely we got under way and carried the summit of the climb without further ado. If the rails had been at all greasy with oil or autumn leaf fall, we'd have stood no chance.

Our recording work done, Karl and I sat in the rear cab to study this curious branch that had managed to escape the clutches of Beeching (and others). Imagine any leafy country lane but with a railway track in the middle of it and you'll get the picture. The Calstock viaduct in particular is a marvellous structure that would have served to hasten the closure of any other line like this, were it not for the special circumstances that apparently pertain in that area; in short, no obvious alternative road journey for a bus service.

The next two days involved very early starts, the sort that everyone dreads as if you do manage to get any sleep, it's never enough and you need to rise at a time when your body expects to be in its deepest sleep. It's also likely to be cold and there's no cooked breakfast to look forward to either! I do remember the spectacular view from the train, though, as we headed west away from the rising sun, the early morning mist settled like puddles of water in the valley bottoms below us as we ran high above them on embankments and viaducts. Tuesday saw us recording back to Truro and doing the Falmouth Docks branch. Then it was back through Plymouth to Newton Abbot and the Paignton line, finishing off with the Heathfield branch, which hadn't seen any traffic in months, if not years. A local track engineer joined us for that, although I got the impression that there was no particular interest in the state of the

Right: Having recorded down to the limit of the branch at Monk Bretton, TRU had to wait some time for its next path at Oakenshaw South Junction. Passing below on the main line, we see a Voyager DMU heading for Leeds. A winter addition of a yellow plastic coupling cover ensures that the train doesn't disgrace itself in the colder weather. 9 December 2011.

Below: What a lot of tracks there are in Drax Power Station! TRU is shown traversing track F and not going through the unloaders. On another occasion, with TIC and top and tail Class 31s, we were barred from entering the site and just recorded the Drax branch itself. 24 August 2010.

I rather like this image of the TRU at Ilkley station: A Beeching-era survivor (and I certainly don't blame him for ALL rail closures in the 1960s), this is an attractive little terminus. Someone has a tall stepladder for attending to the lighting while two youngsters patrol the opposite platform on their scooters. The black and white stickers on the front of the train were for the setting up of the cameras used on video survey work. 25 August 2010.

track. Perhaps we were going to be the last train down there as it was certainly very overgrown at the far end. On a subsequent visit I found that this branch recording had been dropped from the schedule, although it did end up seeing some timber traffic after that.

Subsequent spells I had on the unit were in the North East and to the far north of Scotland. The latter started with a very long transit move from Derby via the Highland Main Line, punctuated with a couple of short recoveries of track that had been missed on a previous recording run. Once north of Inverness, we found ourselves picking up a number of alignment faults on the ageing jointed track that was still a feature of that line at the time. Our portable RETB kit would sometimes struggle to pick up and send signals to the control centre. Therefore, getting permission to enter the next signalling section at certain passing points proved time-consuming as we'd have to set back for a distance and then run forward again until the codes had been completely sent. After we'd been to the Kyle and a return trip to Aberdeen, it was time for us to hand over to a relief crew and I returned home from Inverness by service train.

In regard to the freight-only lines that TRU had to record, there were some where it was practically impossible to book any path and night running wasn't an option without getting signal boxes opened up specially for us; that entailed extra expense. Quite often freight trains (coal, especially) operated according to demand and negotiations with the freight operators were an ongoing affair – they wanted the freedom to plan their trains whenever they wanted but if our monitoring trains couldn't run within a certain timescale the track engineers would start to impose speed restrictions. Or even line closures.

Pending my move to an office job (not half as enjoyable) in Milton Keynes, I came off my regular work on NMT. On 5 December 2011 it was an early start from the yard at Derby again but this time, my colleague Russ (Rusty) Licence had everything powered up and TRU was nice and warm to be in, just how it should be. In fact, I'm glad he'd got there before me as the train was groaning with new kit, some of which I'd never seen before; so I had a little learning (and relearning) process to go through on the transit to the Holmes Chord in Yorkshire before driver Richard Waterhouse handed over to Jason Rogers, who was our lead man for most of the week. Typically, the TRU would visit areas such as South/West Yorkshire and the North East twice each year, covering a selection of routes in those areas on the first visit and then doing the remainder on the second visit. The aim was not to overload the local maintenance units with a long list of track faults that needed attention within the fourteen days that followed (the period within which faults had to be corrected, depending upon their severity). Usually, both the up and down lines would be checked on any double-track section on the same day, anything to make life a bit easier for the track engineers.

Whereas when I first worked TRU, the only task was track geometry recording, now there were several data flows to collect: straight ahead HD video from the central camera in each cab (recorded on to hard drives now, rather than video tape), rail profile measurements (from the KLD laser system), Ground-Penetrating Radar (GPR) scans and Real Time Positioning System (RTPS) plots to feed into the next version of the national digital map (which would assist in abolishing the use of the RST files that stemmed from earlier track recording days). A newly developing geometry system (supplied by Balfour Beatty) was also being tested by running in parallel with the existing Serco-Lewis system. All of these systems required stopping and starting whenever the train made a reversal. As the

GPR system was located in the other vehicle, someone would have to charge down the corridor to make the required mouse clicks before the driver had walked through to change ends and was ready to go again! In fact, most things were better from the driver's point of view when driving TRU, rather than a loco, not least the ability to quickly change ends in the warm and dry and collect a fresh mug of tea or coffee on the way!

The week passed relatively uneventfully this time and with some better weather. With the early starts, breakfast in our hotels was missed each day, of course, so thank goodness for the station cafés at Huddersfield and Bridlington, as well as Greggs in the Doncaster shopping centre (where the station buffet wasn't open until 0730 – shameful!). Modest though they were, our on-train facilities proved their worth on the other days.

With my time on the trains coming to a close, I made sure I got some shots of the unit on the Lynemouth branch because the aluminium smelter plant it served was soon to close. The following day, as we ran along the coastal stretch of the line to the potash mines at Hunt Cliff, I recalled Michael Portillo mentioning on one of his TV programmes that he wished he could witness that view!

Now this is one photo that I would never have considered taking had I still been using film. I've dialled in 1000ASA and taken it at 1/30sec @ f2.8, if I remember correctly, to let in as much light as possible. The TRU driver is probably thinking I'm bonkers but you have to try these things sometimes – monitoring trains have rarely visited Redditch in daylight, so it had to be done! 10 August 2010.

Not so far from Redditch; all platforms are occupied at Stratford upon Avon ... and all by the same type of train. No. 950001 meets 150108 and 150132 amidst the snow and ice of one of the coldest Decembers the country had seen for many years. In the background, construction had begun on a new station footbridge. 21 December 2010.

'Poets Corner' says the road sign beyond but we weren't really in the mood for poetry. It had been a long day; everyone was ready for a hot meal at the hotel and early to bed but because of frozen points, TRU was having to wait at Small Heath before it could go on to Tyseley depot. Driver Mike Jones waits for the call! 20 December 2010.

The Present and the Future?

U pon leaving my role as an on-train technician, I followed the fortunes of the IM fleet with interest. Having been lucky enough to be sponsored by Network Rail to study for a foundation degree in Railway Engineering at Sheffield Hallam University, I moved to the position of fleet engineer, which sometimes enabled me to carry out work connected with the test trains.

The biggest change was undoubtedly the development and phased introduction of Plain Line Pattern Recognition (PLPR). One of the items of kit trialled on the NMT was the Cybernetix system, an arrangement of cameras mounted underneath the train to record images of the track itself at line speed. Although that particular set-up didn't move into production, a similar system was developed by Omnicom that

My fellow OTT, Dave Curran, chats to driver Sean Dunne before we prep a set including TIC, RSC1 and EMV (977983) at Bramdean Sidings (near Hither Green). The lead loco is 73107 *Redhill 1844–1994* with 73138 at the rear and we will run down to Dover, finishing at London Victoria sometime in the afternoon. I would operate the Conductor Rail Monitoring system on EMV. 30 September 2011.

Opposite top: Aylesbury is very much a DMU stronghold so seeing a locomotive-hauled train rolling in there in perfect lighting conditions has to be a rarity. An additional run on a Sunday has been deemed necessary here, probably due to a previous cancelled or curtailed shift (on different timings) that has produced an urgent need to collect data on the Chiltern route if speed restrictions aren't to be imposed. PLPR4 (72639) is performing the honours, together with its usual companion TIC2 (977974) in the centre, plus Mentor (975091), which I'm guessing is providing extra braking force as the generator in TIC2 appears to be running. No. 37610 *T.S. (Ted) Cassady 14.5.61–6.4.08* leads while 37606 trails. 3 May 2015.

Opposite bottom: Doing the ton through Milton Keynes, 67020 and 030 are trying to keep to NMT timings with a PLPR set on the WCML up fast with driver Dave Talbot at the helm. Generator coach 6263 is the first vehicle, providing electrical power to the train. 10 September 2014.

Above: PLPR2 (5981) sits in platform 6 at Euston between DVT 82145 and 67012 *A Shropshire Lad.* Very popular with the drivers, NR's new fleet of DVTs had been cleared to operate this particular WCML run out of Derby but little else. With the contract for operating IM Fleet trains passing to Colas, efforts to widen their acceptance seemed to fade and they spent most of their time out of use at the RTC. All PLPR trains required two-loco operation as a result, with short sets like this one no longer appearing. 14 April 2015.

grew into PLPR. The big 'win' with PLPR, from a staff safety angle at least, was to substantially reduce the need for staff to undertake the regular track walking known as BVI (Basic Visual Inspection). Not aimed at assessing track geometry, this task involved checking for loose or missing rail clips, damaged sleepers or other track components. It relied upon the diligence of the inspectors and if it was conducted on lines open to traffic, it put them in some degree of danger. On busier routes, line possessions might be required and that was becoming less acceptable. In the longer term, also less acceptable was the pounding that the hips and knees of track walkers were taking from being on the ballast. The phased introduction of

PLPR changed that and with the very high frequency of image recording and use of proven object recognition software, a more consistent, quicker and safer system of track inspection is now in place. 'Candidate' track faults are now flagged up to the track inspector in a safe office environment alongside associated track geometry information, which can lead to a more informed assessment of the fault. The only problem unaddressed is if the track should be covered in deep snow, but that's no different to before! In addition to the NMT, there are now four PLPR coaches in operation across the country (Mark 2s 72631, 5981, 1256 and 72639) with all routes that are laid with CWR to be covered by them.

Above: In the summer of 2014, the Production and Development Vehicles were both removed from the NMT set for major overhaul. However, instead of running a loco-hauled set in its place (as was normal practice) a hybrid formation was devised using the NMT power cars for traction. This mix of Mark 1, 2 and 3 coaches didn't seem to grab the headlines much but I made sure I got some photos of it. I believe it was limited to 90mph running so whether anything similar will appear again remains to be seen. Mentor 975091 is in the middle of the formation here (pantograph raised), though a Mark 2 was later put in its place. Annoyingly, I didn't record the full set of vehicle numbers but I believe they are 975984, 72616, 975091, 5981, 9516 and 977984 (43013 tailing); OHL monitoring would clearly be happening in Mentor and PLPR/track geometry monitoring being undertaken in 5981 (PLPR2). No. 43014 *The Railway Observer* leads the train through Cheddington with Tony Falloon driving, Driver Manager Dave Talbot alongside him has spotted me! 22 July 2014.

Opposite top: Just to show how the NMT looks today: The lining along the centre of the train has gone and been replaced with some corporate promotion! All three power cars now carry names. No. 43014 is seen passing by Cockwood Harbour forming 1Z18 1546 Paignton–Taunton with 43062 at the rear. 23 September 2016.

Opposite bottom: The contract for operating Network Rail's IM fleet passed to Colas but in 2016, newly introduced Class 68s operated by DRS were employed on some PLPR trains, until Colas obtained its own two Class 67s. In place of the NMT, 68021 *Tireless* and 68005 *Avenger* top and tail a set that includes 'Mentor' with its pantograph raised as 1Q27 1229 Crewe L&NWR–Derby RTC (via Euston) at Old Linslade. The NMT undergoes a week of maintenance periodically and the running of a PLPR set in its place on the WCML provides an opportunity to use Mentor to monitor the OLE. 14 September 2016.

This brings me to the forgotten test train: DR98008 is a Network Rail MPV supplied by Windhoff, unique in the country's fleet in having twin cabs mounted on a single vehicle (the rest are single-cabbed, like an HST power car). It has been kitted out with the OmniInspector system; track inspection imaging equipment that works similarly to PLPR but intended for use in complex station areas or junctions. As with PLPR, this is intended to reduce or replace the need to send people out on to the track to make detailed inspections. Like the UTUs, it tends to do its work at night but is sometimes seen making transit moves by day. It may be supplemented by further machines for this work in the future.

Further living up to its role of trialling new kit, NMT was a platform for testing an Unattended Geometry Measurement System (UGMS). This was geometry measurement equipment that was compact enough to be fitted to service trains and require minimal attention in order to acquire dynamic track geometry data. The long-term aim was to reduce and eventually eliminate the need to run special trains for this purpose, the latter being something

No. 43062 with its smoky Paxman Valenta power unit ticks over inside Craigentinny's main inspection shed, an appropriate scene with which to end this book. 9 January 2006.

of a dream for some within Network Rail; it would free up paths on the network and maybe save the company some money in the process, whoopee!

Calm down. To achieve that would require a considerable number of passenger trains across many operators to be fitted with UGMS kits, so that you were certain of acquiring data often enough for every stretch of operational track to satisfy the track engineers. However, that obviously wouldn't cover freight-only routes, plus you'd need to be sure that all the kits were properly calibrated and maintained to ensure accuracy. Perhaps the financial savings might not be so great, with UGMS-derived data being seen as an add-on to that from the regular runs of geometry assessment test trains. Current technology in ultrasonics would seem to require UTU trains to carry on their slow-speed monitoring for the foreseeable future, even if the other IM functions' equipment might get adopted in compact form by service trains.

When I joined Serco to work on the NMT, the declaration made at the time was that for track maintenance issues, overall the industry was looking to move from a 'find and fix' mentality to one of 'predict and prevent'. The first approach clearly meant that track faults could only be addressed when they were found and depended very much on the frequency of inspection being sufficient to detect any before they deteriorated to a dangerous state. The latter approach involved better analysis of data with an increase in inspection frequency to the point where it could be predicted where track faults were more likely to develop. Track maintenance effort could then be stepped up in those areas so that faults never got the chance to become dangerous. While progress was certainly made, perhaps this state of affairs has proved somewhat harder to achieve than first thought as quite recently I heard higher management calling for a move to 'predict and prevent'! All in all, I would expect to see a continuing presence of monitoring trains on the network for some years to come.

On a final note, I suggested to the Data Services department that they might like to give a new name to the NMT (and maybe put an end to those arguments over the use of the word 'new'!). In the manner of 'Mentor', I thought that 'Talisman' would be a good name for it: Testing And Line Inspection Special; Monitoring Across the Network.

The name has a railway pedigree after all and a talisman is a good luck charm, so I thought the name would be appropriate for applying to Network Rail's flagship. If it ever happens, just remember who thought of it first!

Index

Caption references are in *italics*.